This item was purchased for the Library
through Zip Books, a statewide project of
the NorthNet Library System, funded by
the California State Library.

Praise for *Raising White Kids*

"Required reading. This astounding book has a real shot of changing the conversation on race in America. If you're white and have a kid (or have ever been a kid), please read this book."
—**Saira Rao**, co-founder, In This Together Media

"*Raising White Kids* is both an antidote to the racial ignorance and fear most white families unknowingly pass along to their young and a powerful way to call white adults into the process of racial awakening in the name of creating more just and functional communities for all. Buy this book for yourself, for your children's teachers, and for all parents and grandparents of white children who you know."
—**Debby Irving**, author *Waking Up White, and Finding Myself in the Story of Race*

"Jennifer Harvey's brilliant work and passion for racial justice come alive on every page. *Raising White Kids* is a theory-rich, practical guide with wonderfully helpful examples that will equip parents to navigate today's racial challenges with confidence and grace. For the millions of mothers and fathers who are deeply invested in creating a better tomorrow in an increasingly multicultural America, Harvey's book couldn't be more helpful or more needed right now."
—**Diana Butler Bass**, author of *Grateful: The Transformative Power of Giving Thanks*

"Jennifer Harvey's *Dear White Christians* was a wakeup call to white congregations whose good intentions were often undermined by their own blind spots. With *Raising White Kids*, Harvey offers a much-needed roadmap for white parents who realize that racial injustice isn't just a problem for kids of color. This insightful and practical book is a must-read for white parents who want to raise surefooted, self-aware kids in an increasingly diverse America. There are few things more important to the future of our democracy."
—**Robert P. Jones**, CEO, Public Religion Research Institute, and author of *The End of White Christian America*

"Finally! Jennifer Harvey provides a long-awaited and much-needed answer to a question often posed by white antiracist allies: How do we raise our children to be allies in the struggle against racism? *Raising White Kids* provides practical advice and examples for parents that are well-grounded in the scholarship on racial identity and racial socialization. It would be a mistake, however, to think that this book is only for parents of white children. It is a critical resource for educators whose efforts to teach about racial oppression are routinely hampered by the wide knowledge gap between white students and students of color. Harvey helps faculty to understand why white students often need intense remediation around issues of race and racism, and provides both faculty and students with language and tools to grapple with the culture shock that comes with learning about racism for the first time."
—**Chanequa Walker-Barnes**, PhD, Associate Professor of Practical Theology, McAfee School of Theology

"*Raising White Kids* asks parents to reconsider the conventional yet failed strategies of promoting colorblindness and valuing diversity (without addressing whiteness), which prove inadequate in the face of our racial crisis by ignoring or white-washing racial difference. Instead, Harvey proposes a 'race-conscious' approach to raising white children that helps children not only to perceive racism in ways a colorblind approach veils but also to contest racism through directly engaging with children about race and racial injustice—early and often. Combining research on child development with her extensive scholarship on racial formation and practices of antiracism, Harvey has written an easily readable book full of examples and concrete practices that helps parents give their children the tools they need to develop a healthy white racial identity. *Raising White Kids* is urgent, important, and practical reading for anyone involved in the rearing of white children."
—**Dr. Kristopher Norris**, Visiting Distinguished Professor of Public Theology at Wesley Theological Seminary, Washington, DC.

FOREWORD BY **TIM WISE**

Author of *White Like Me: Reflections on Race from a Privileged Son*

RAISING WHITE KIDS

BRINGING UP CHILDREN
IN A **RACIALLY UNJUST AMERICA**

JENNIFER HARVEY

ABINGDON PRESS
NASHVILLE

RAISING WHITE KIDS

BRINGING UP CHILDREN IN A RACIALLY UNJUST AMERICA

Copyright © 2017 by Jennifer Harvey

All rights reserved.

Library of Congress Cataloging-in-Publication Data has been requested.

ISBN 978-1-5018-5642-6

18 19 20 21 22 23 24 25—10 9 8 7 6 5 4 3

MANUFACTURED IN THE UNITED STATES OF AMERICA

For my nephews, A. and T.

I think that the hard work of a nonracist sensibility is the boundary crossing, from safe circle into wilderness: the testing of boundary, the consecration of sacrilege. It is the willingness to spoil a good party and break an encompassing circle, to travel from the safe to the unsafe. The transgression is dizzyingly intense, a reminder of what it is to be alive.

—*Patricia J. Williams*, The Alchemy of Race and Rights (1991)

Contents

Foreword

Raising children would be difficult enough, even in a nation that wasn't beset by deep and persistent racial inequities. As a father of two teenage daughters, I sometimes marvel at how my wife and I have managed to get them to this point without too much observable damage (at least yet!). Navigating the vagaries of parenting even in the best of worlds takes time, more energy than one can often imagine, and a reserve of patience that can wear thin as we try to balance the responsibilities of work and home. But when we add layer upon layer of societal injustice ingrained over generations to the everyday challenges presented by the rearing of kids—and the mentalities that too often become enshrined as rationalizations for those injustices—the job becomes infinitely harder.

Obviously, these difficulties present most viscerally for parents of color. They are the ones who have to have "the talk" with their children about police and traffic stops and keeping one's hands on the wheel lest one become another headline, another statistic. It is their children who, like Tamir Rice, can be gunned down by an officer in a public park while playing with a toy gun: something white parents let their boys do every day without ever thinking twice about it. They are the ones who have to worry about whether teachers will see their child's full potential or instead view them through the lens of debilitating group stereotypes, sending them down a road that for too many becomes a school-to-prison pipeline. For most white parents these daily and quite normative concerns for black and brown parents are abstractions. Even when we hear these kinds of parenting stories repeated time and again, perhaps by colleagues or friends of color—and even if we reject the common tendency among white folks to think people of color are exaggerating the problems of racial mistreatment—it's easy to wonder what any of this has to do with us or the way that *we* parent.

But of course, if some in our nation are being profiled by law enforcement, tracked into lower-level academic classes, and viewed as potential troublemakers at least from their pre-teen years onward, then others of us—in this case, white others—are typically being elevated, are being given a pass, are being tracked high and viewed as capable of doing whatever we might desire. In short, our white children are being racialized every bit as much as children of color. There is no down without an up, no underprivilege without overprivilege, no disadvantage without advantage. And when one's white kids are being raised with various forms of advantage—though I realize these can often be mediated by class, gender, sexuality, disability, and other confounding identities—white parents have to take special care to navigate the waters of that racialization with intentionality. Ignoring it, or raising those children not to "see color" or notice difference or to believe that "we're all the same" and should treat everyone as such, is to ill-prepare our white children to confront the inequities that persist. You can't fix a problem you refuse to face, and you won't likely commit to fixing it if you're unclear of where you fit in the racialized order of America—and why and how you got there.

This is why Jennifer Harvey's work in this volume is so important. She understands the complexities of raising white kids in a society that was literally created for them. Specifically, she recognizes how hard it can be to raise them empathetically and as allies in the struggle for justice when everything around them encourages a passive acceptance (or maybe even active hoarding) of the advantages of birth. This is no small feat. Just as raising boys to resist the easy lures of casual sexism (and even deep-seated misogyny) is difficult in a society of male dominance, so too raising white children not to blindly accept the systemic benefits of institutionalized white supremacy, and to even challenge the system that bestows them, is a monumental task. But herein, Harvey shows that with the proper commitment, a true understanding of our own racialization, a humility that allows us to listen and learn, and a willingness to make mistakes, white parents can be up to the task. And importantly, we can do it without instilling unproductive guilt in our kids. In fact, we can help them build up a new and empowering identity as antiracist white allies.

Not only *can* we do this; we must. Our children are learning white supremacy every day and in many different ways. They can see inequities with their own eyes, and they don't need a college degree to start wondering what those inequities mean. They can see the conditions in this neighborhood versus that one, or in the schools they attend by and large versus the ones attended by black and brown kids. They can see who's being arrested on the evening news, and who isn't. And in a society that is teaching them every day, "you can be anything you want if you just try hard," is it any wonder that many of them might then internalize the notion that white folks like themselves really are smarter, harder working, or more law-abiding? Children are not born with a sociological imagination, but they are born with lots of curiosity. Unless we meet their curiosity with the context necessary for making sense of the world around them, and understanding the inequities they can all too readily observe, they may well default to the position that those disparities are natural, normal, and justifiable. We cannot do that to our children, we must not. To allow the atrophying of their consciences by way of our passivity is to fail as parents.

And frankly, if parents of color have to deal with these things, then who are we to opt out? If children of color have to understand what their color means, and how to live *anyway*, then so must ours. Because in a nation that has shown repeatedly how little it values black and brown life, things will not change unless we make it so. Justice is not an act of wish fulfillment but the product of resistance. Black and brown parents know these things like they know their names, and as a matter of survival they make sure their children know them too. And if their children have to know them, then *ours* must know them as well. If their children are to be allowed no innocence free from these concerns, then so too must ours sacrifice some of their naiveté upon the altar of truth.

Jennifer Harvey is the truth, and we owe her a debt of gratitude for what follows in these pages.

Tim Wise
Nashville, November 2017

GOOD PARENTS, HARD CONVERSATIONS

Standing outside the bathroom at Stedman Elementary where I was in first grade, my friend J. walked up to me. "You know, Jenny," she said. "We should start a white girls club." I must have looked as confused as I felt, because she continued, "You know. Because there are only six white girls in this class."

I had never before considered such a thing. Now, I looked down at my arm. And for the first time in my six years of life it occurred to me that's exactly what I was: a white girl. This new recognition started to wash over me. But I had no time to think about what it might mean before we were sharply interrupted.

"Girls, that's enough!" snapped Ms. B., our teacher who had overheard our exchange. Then more fiercely, "I don't ever want to hear you talk like that again!"

At such a young age, having had not a single adult talk openly about race and its potential meanings in my

1

life, I had no clue what J. and I had done wrong that afternoon. But I knew we had said or done something very, very wrong. More important, I was so ashamed by the rebuke we received from Ms. B. (also white)—a teacher I adored—that I was determined to not go near that something again.

The United States is on a rapid path of becoming one of the most racially diverse nations in the world. It's also a nation full of racial tension. These two realities existing at the same time creates a challenging paradox for parents who want to equip their children to be active and able participants in a multiracial, pluralistic society.

The difficulties faced by parents of white children, however, are different from those faced by parents of children of color. That truth is not something we talk about very often in public conversations about race. But it's true nonetheless. Being committed to equity and justice while living in a society that is not only racially unjust and deeply segregated, but which privileges your racial group at the same time, creates unique conundrums for white people. These conundrums begin early in life and impact the racial development of white children in powerful ways.

How should parents best navigate the many complex situations race creates for us? Should we teach our children to be "color-blind"? Or should we teach them to notice race (and, if so, how)? What strategies will help our children learn to function well in a diverse nation? What roles do we want them to play in addressing racism when they encounter it? How do we equip them for these roles? How do we talk about race honestly with our children, which means naming white privilege as well as many hard truths about what white people have done, without making our children feel bad about being white? Most important, how do we do any of this in age-appropriate ways?

There are so many questions here. But as difficult as these questions are, they bring into view issues parents need to engage with intention and care if we are raising white children. These questions were important since long before the civil rights movement. But the last three years in the United States have made it painfully obvious that they are urgent for the good of this nation and our collective future as a society.

Racial Tension in the United States

Many US Americans were stunned when they woke up to the news the morning of August 10, 2014. Ferguson, Missouri, a suburb of St. Louis most of us had never heard of, was engulfed in chaos. In the weeks that followed, the images that poured out of Ferguson—of fire, smoke, protests, riot-geared police, and young people fleeing tear gas—were almost indistinguishable from those that poured out of Selma, Alabama, in 1965, or Detroit, Michigan, in 1967.

Ferguson didn't come out of nowhere, and it's not as if we've had peace and justice from the late 1960s until now. I vividly remember waking up in Santa Barbara, California, to news coming out of Los Angeles in the early 1990s. Only two hours south of where I was a college student, swaths of the city had erupted in rebellion after an all-white jury exonerated the police officers who had brutally beaten Rodney King, despite their violence having been caught on tape. I remember joining the thousands upon thousands who poured into the New York City streets in 1999 after four police officers killed Amadou Diallo—an unarmed Bronx resident coming peacefully home after a long day's work—in a hail of forty-one bullets. These officers, too, were declared not guilty.

But in the years since Ferguson, pervasive racial tension in the United States has been exposed at new levels. A steady stream of incidents involving police officers killing unarmed African American men and children have continued to flood public awareness. Racial divisions between whites and Blacks, but also between whites and other whites, have intensified. Public debate over the meanings of such deaths has been rancorous, with the gap between those who see such killings as racially motivated and those who do not deep, wide, and polarized.

> Others can't figure out if they're supposed to notice race (that is, value diversity) or be color-blind (that is, not see it).

The turmoil is palpable. In the summer of 2015 nine African American Christians in Charleston, South Carolina, were massacred by a young white man during a Bible study in their church. A national discussion ensued over the presence of the Confederate flag at the South Carolina courthouse. Then, in 2016, in one summer week police killed two Black men as videotape rolled, communities across

4

the nation erupted in furious protest, and a sniper killed seven police officers at a massive, peaceful rally in Dallas, Texas. That same summer we were a year into a presidential campaign that was not merely divisive, but which further exacerbated racial tensions and in which accusations of racism came to take center stage.

When the election was over, thousands of people protested the outcome and many of the protests emphasized race. Hundreds of high school students, many too young to vote, walked out of school to denounce the rhetoric of the president-elect with chants of "No justice, no peace!" "Black Lives Matter," and "Undocumented and unafraid!" Schools reported an uptick in racial harassment. White students made jokes to Latino/a students about the deportations to come or—as a teacher friend of mine experienced in his school in Iowa—mused within earshot of African American students as to whether the election means "we get to have slavery again."

Racial trouble—violence, division, mistrust, and unrest—is alive and well. It will surely remain so for some time to come.

For many white US Americans, this turmoil has generated an acute awareness of how much work remains undone. Many of these same folks, whites who are committed to equality, are eager to be part of solutions to our racial trouble. At the same time, many of us are not sure what to do. The question "What do we do?" has been asked by equality-committed white people with increasing frequency in public discussions about race since we woke up to Ferguson. This book offers one constructive response to that question.

The response *Raising White Kids* offers is very specific. At the very least, the current racial crisis has made clear that the strategies we have used for a long time in the hopes of creating just and diverse communities have failed us. Among the many arenas of social life in which this question urgently needs to be addressed, a powerful and formative, but easily overlooked one is the arena of raising white children. The difficult reality is this: the dominant strategies the nation as a whole has tried are the same ones that equality- and justice-minded parents of white children have used since the civil rights era in the hope of teaching tolerance, fairness, equality and justice. And, as with the nation as a whole, these strategies have proven themselves inadequate to the task of facing the racial challenges with which we are living in this nation.

This recognition may be difficult to acknowledge. It may even be painful. But it need not be the end of the story. If the tried and true has not worked, then it's time for something new.

Let's Talk About Bringing Up Children

A multiracial group of students sit together in a high school or college classroom. The teacher walks in and says, "Today we're going to start our unit on race." White students who were previously talkative and engaged suddenly become quiet and withdrawn. A few look like deer in headlights.

In more than a decade of teaching ethics to college students, I have seen such fear and silence fall across a college classroom more times than I can count. In fact, my white students find it easier to talk about the controversial topic of abortion than they do race. The students depicted in this classroom story are prime examples of the long-term consequences of adults' inadequate racial engagement with white children.

Parents of Black, Latino/a and other children of color have to teach their children about race as a basic matter of their children's well-being and survival, usually from very young ages.* Consider a micro-level example: hearing a racial epithet on the playground becomes a moment in which these parents have to teach something explicit about race, taking into account their child's age. They must do so even if the children using or hearing the epithet have no clue what it means. Or consider a macro-level example: these same parents know they have to sit their children down and have "the talk" at some point. They have to explain to their children, in the hopes of creating safety,

---

* You may notice that throughout this book, I never capitalize *white* but I always capitalize *Black*. This may seem to be either an unfair, or at least a grammatically inappropriate nonparallel use of racial terms. But white identity and Black identity are not parallels. And while language is never perfect, it's my sense that this is the best way to indicate these different identities. As will become clear in later chapters, African American communities have created Black identity as a conscious, collective, intentional, historical, and constructive way to self-identify. While different writers make different choices, many of the African American thinkers I am most indebted to use Black and not black. In contrast, to this point in US racial history, white is not a similarly constructive, conscious, and collective identity that has been claimed— at least not for the purposes of antiracism. Thus, I always indicate white with the lowercase *w*.

7

how to conduct themselves if or when they encounter police.

In countless day-to-day life moments, parents of children of color make difficult choices about when, what, and how much to say. They consider how to be effective in making their children aware of US racial realities and dangers, while simultaneously nurturing their children's emotional resilience and a healthy sense of racial identity. They navigate a difficult path: not damaging their child's psyche by causing him/her to internalize the notion that because others perceive or treat him/her negatively there must, in fact, be something negative about themselves, without sugarcoating the truth that their children will experience racialized and racist encounters as they go about their daily lives. To sugarcoat leaves their children more vulnerable than they already are.

Such nuanced, complex, challenging conversations are a fundamental necessity of parenting children of color. No obvious parallels exist for white families. As a result, racial conversations in white families tend to be one-dimensional.

In contrast to "the talk," for example, a one-dimensional teaching becomes "police are safe; go find one if you are in trouble." In contrast to "we should all be equal, we all have equal worth, but we don't yet all experience equality," a one-dimensional teaching becomes "we are all equal."

The relatively poor quality of racial conversations between white parents and their children is a key reason my white students look like deer in headlights. For white students in my college classroom the fear is different from what students of color may experience. Because, prior to this point, they are less likely to have been actively nurtured in their understanding of race and its meaning in their lives, white students are generally far, far behind their peers of color. Their racial understanding is underdeveloped, at best, deeply confused at worst. Their experience is something like having only ever been taught basic addition and suddenly being thrown into a calculus class.

Imagine being told your entire life that the most important thing you need to know about race in your daily life experience is that "we're all equal." Then, imagine being suddenly expected at the age of nineteen to make sense out of a news story coming out of Ferguson, let alone be an informed and able discussant in a high school or college classroom about social realities that make clear *such equality is actually not the case*. Some of these white students struggle to hear their peers' life experiences or engage data about race in the United States because they have only been taught that we're all, at core, the same. Some of them are afraid to talk because they worry they'll say something racist. This is understandable. They've had little practice talking about race openly. Some believe they have little to offer to the conversation. Others can't figure out if they're supposed to notice race (that is, value diversity) or be color-blind (that is, not see it).

These students are justified in all of this worry and confusion. After all, a child who's only been taught addition *is* going to fail calculus! By being placed in such a class unequipped, that child has been set up by adults to fail.

Meanwhile, the harms caused by inadequate attention to the development of white racial identity in our children's lives

9

run even deeper than the fears that show up in this classroom discussion. These same young people are often aware that racial tensions exist. Many of them know or sense that these tensions have to do with injustices white people have committed. Such awareness—combined with the absence of nuanced, supportive, complex discussions—has long since impacted these young white people. It shows up as anxiety, guilt, cognitive dissonance, or even anger when race does come up. White youth struggle to find or experience a truly meaningful place from which to participate fully in conversations about diversity and multiculturalism, even while they get pressure from adults to do so as they grow older.

> Racial development is no different than physical, intellectual, or emotional development.

On top of all of this, that whites are behind when it comes to race makes racial tensions worse. For example, when these same white students are reluctant to talk about, are ill-equipped to understand, or show anxiety and resistance to honest engagement with race, students of color in the room get the message that their white peers just don't care. Such white reactions are just further evidence to them that most white people are, in fact, "racist."

Whether or not this is a fair interpretation is irrelevant. The impact of such a perception is profound. Students of color become frustrated and angry that their white peers won't engage. Their frustration is understandable given the extent to which racism is a life-or-death social reality for them. Meanwhile, most students of color have lots of firsthand experience by the age of nineteen that makes it safe to presume whites don't and don't really want to understand the realities they face. At the end of the day, one disastrous result of white people being so far behind is deeper racial alienation and greater misunderstanding still.

So Now What?

The questions that became more obviously urgent beginning in the fall of 2014 weren't actually new. Race in the United States has long been loaded. My childhood experience with Ms. B. illustrates just how loaded race can be. That experience also illustrates how powerfully adults' engagement impacts children.

Ms. B.'s response to me and my friend J. came from a well-intentioned place. She was afraid something "bad" was going on. The exchange she overheard sounded to her like J. and I were making observations that were, or had the potential to become, racist.

As an educator and a white American who valued equality, Ms. B. was right to intervene in a six-year-old reasoning process that (1) noticed race and (2) concluded racial difference is a good reason to stick with one's own kind. But her desire to make clear that what we were contemplating was unacceptable was accompanied by so much anxiety that Ms. B. silenced what was actually a developmentally innocent exploration. Her failure to come back later and help us understand why it so upset her made that silence even worse.

Ironically, Ms. B.'s response made more likely the very results she was hoping to avoid. Her reaction transmitted adult racial tension to J. and me. Without age-appropriate support to understand, we became vulnerable to internalizing this tension. We became likely to learn that staying on our "side" of the racial divide was the safest thing to do. We became unlikely to engage adults with our questions, experiences, and observations about race. In this, as in so many other transactions like it, such teachings are transmitted without any racial words being used by the adult at all.

It's not exactly that our experience made J. and me more likely to become racist. But we learned clearly that something hard, bad, even scary hovered around this issue of skin color and difference. And that learning, over time, translates into behavior that looks like—or may become or cause—racial division, tension, or even overt racism.

This story surfaces one of the challenges that exist in the racially fraught moments parents (and teachers and other important caregivers) may encounter with children of diverse racial groups and identities. Many parents recognize and experience these challenges. Indeed, few parents can fail to identify with the anxiety of being in Ms. B.'s shoes. But we may not realize that ineffective handling of many small racial encounters like this one, over time, has very serious long-term consequences.

Whether they begin as early (or even earlier) as first grade in an encounter outside a lavatory, or show up, predictably, among white college students, such cycles and dynamics need not remain as they are. White parents have significant power to positively intervene in and fundamentally change them.

Racial development is no different than physical, intellectual, or emotional development. Children develop physically, intellectually, or emotionally regardless of what kind of attention their parents offer them. But the outcomes are dramatically different depending on the kind of attention they are given. So it is with racial development, which takes place whether parents nurture it or not. In terms of racial development, then, the one-dimensional conversations that tend to take place in white households are the equivalent of having offered our children sugar ("we're all the same underneath our skin") when they need protein- and vitamin-rich food ("we believe in equality and it's important to figure out how to stand up for that when it's not there").

But parents today may have been raised on Frosted Flakes and still decide to learn about nutrition and commit to healthier eating once they have had children. We who are parents of white children can similarly learn about racial development and commit to practices that offer racial nurture. We can come to understand the urgency of offering our children the tools they need to develop a healthy white racial identity. We can learn how to actually offer them. *Raising White Kids* is a book that supports such parents in doing so.

We face difficult and complex racial realities in this nation today. The challenges will not be overcome quickly or with one dramatic solution. It will certainly take more than different parenting strategies in white families to create a just racial future.

It will take more than courageous teachers engaging race and racism directly with their young students. We have a very long way to go. But the practices explored in this book can move us a significant distance in the right direction. In other words, we may have far to go, but *we can go*.

What to Expect from This Book

It's probably already obvious that I wrote *Raising White Kids* primarily with parents in mind. Part of the reason I did so is because of my own journey. I've worked on and for antiracism and the role of white people in it for a long time. But becoming a parent changed so much about what I thought I knew. I realized how few of the strategies I relied on helped me engage my children, and how many new strategies I desperately needed. Meanwhile, I'm also aware that parents and primary caretakers really are on the front lines in terms of the most urgent and difficult dimensions of bringing up white children in a racially unjust nation. Day in and day out, children in our lives are learning about race, and we must be ready to engage them if we want them to learn the right things.

> Why not all kids? Shouldn't racial justice matters address everybody?

Yet I've also learned a lot about youth, whiteness, and antiracism through my work as a teacher. And I know the impact teachers can have. In addition, children are deeply and powerfully impacted by an array of beloved adults besides parents. Godparents, aunts, uncles, grandparents, religious education teachers, and so many others bear an important responsibility when it comes to bringing up white children for racial justice. All of us who are adults can make a significant and positive impact in the lives of white children who are not our own.

So the focus of this book and the language primarily used within it refers to *parents*. At the same time, I'm clear this book is potentially meaningful for anyone who has children in their lives (including children of color who may themselves have white friends) and I've written it with that awareness. The working principles and many of the examples shared here are easily applied to a variety of adult-children relationships. It's just as vital that any adult committed to racial justice who has significant relationships with white children learn these approaches as it is for their parents. It also may be the case that parents who engage the content here will find they want to share this book with other adults who have relationships with their own children.

At this point, yet a different matter in terms of reader expectations needs to be addressed. It may be the case, in fact, that the specificity of this book—raising *white* kids—already raised a few eyebrows. Why not all kids? Shouldn't racial justice matters address everybody?

The reality is that the challenges addressed and insights offered here simply can't be generalized. They just don't apply in the same way to *all* children. (The reasons this is the case will become more obvious the farther we go.) Because the quandaries of being white are different than those posed by being of color, therefore, this book is written specifically for parents of white children, and other caregivers and teachers involved in bringing up white kids.

But the larger truth is that committing to nurturing healthy white racial identity is not ultimately about or for the good of white children only. When we bring up white children—who grow to be white teenagers, twentysomethings, full-blown adults—who are able, engaged, and high-functioning when it comes to matters of race, diversity, and, most important, anti-racism, we are parenting in ways that are good for everyone's children.

Raising White Kids takes on the two approaches to race that impact the ways adults engage white children the most: that is, strategies of color-blindness and diversity. It explains precisely why color-blind teaching, the most prevalent approach, has failed. It pays attention to the kinds of anxieties that overt discussions of race (like those seen in my encounter with Ms. B.) elicit in white adults. It points out the silence and silencing responses that both cause color-blind teaching, as well as becoming the outcomes to which color-blind teaching leads.

This book also explores the complexities that exist when we teach white children they should value diversity. Diversity approaches have not overtaken color-blindness as the dominant approach to race. But a focus on diversity has been on the rise in recent years, especially in schools. Teaching children they should embrace and celebrate difference—or "value diversity"—is a significant improvement over color-blind teaching. But it, too, is inadequate, largely because it doesn't address some of the unique issues faced by whites when we move past color-blindness.

For example, I've heard countless parents attempting to engage issues of race with their children share experiences and concerns such as these:

"I worry about what to say to my second-grader about racism. He has lots of Black friends. I don't want him to start to treat them as being somehow different. I also don't want to say something to him about racism that then he repeats to his friends in a way that hurts them."

"I don't want to lie to my kids about the United States. But how do I talk about its violent history—such as what slavery or treatment of Native Americans was like? I don't even let my kids watch violent TV."

"I've gone out of my way to put my kids in diverse situations their entire lives. And yet the older they've gotten, the whiter their friend group seems to get. I don't really know what's going on, let alone what to do about it."

Each of these concerns is a reflection of the real dilemmas that attend attempts to raise healthy white children in a deeply racialized and hierarchical society.

We want to raise white children who have a good understanding of race and its meanings. We want to raise children who are comfortable in their own skin while simultaneously living authentically in diverse and multicultural spaces. We want our children to be able to contribute productively to making things racially better in the United States. To move closer to all of these things, we have to understand how race and racism impact white children. And we need strategies to respond effectively to complex and challenging racial moments, whether such moments are as obvious as was my own with Ms. B. or so subtle an adult might not even realize, at first, something racial is taking place.

Raising White Kids provides such strategies. It supports parents in developing the broader base of knowledge they need to create their own strategies through various stages of their children's development. Throughout this book, you will find numerous examples of real-life scenarios, as well as numerous real experiences of actual parents and teachers. Some of these experiences were shared with me. Others are experiences I have faced myself in my journey of parenting two young white children (my children are currently under the age of ten).

In place of both color-blindness and diversity teachings this book offers a race-conscious approach to parenting. Race-conscious parenting acknowledges, names, discusses, and otherwise engages racial difference and racial justice with children. It does so early and often. It assumes that antiracism must be a central and deep-seated commitment when it comes to how we parent white children and in what we want them to learn.

You may be familiar with ways of talking about children and racial difference in which the importance of teaching children *not to be racist* is emphasized. This way of thinking usually means trying to prevent the formation of negative stereotypes about people of different races, or undo those that have already been adopted.

But *nonracism* is not the same thing as *antiracism*. It is important to combat stereotypes and biases. But in any context where racism and racial injustice already run rampant, nonracism isn't enough to create equity or justice. In such a context, antiracism is required. A commitment to antiracism goes well beyond nonracism. It means actively countering and challenging racism. And given that racism is, tragically, far too normal and pervasive in the United States, *Raising White Kids* presumes that cultivating antiracism in our children and living it ourselves is a key commitment to bringing up healthy white children in this nation.

The stories I share in this book illustrate the differences between color-blind and race-conscious parental responses. They explore the distinct outcomes to which such distinct responses lead. Sharing them will enable parents to imagine other practical and constructive responses they might enact with their own children in different scenarios and at various ages.

The chapters are not organized by chronological age. Whatever our racial identity, we cycle through various stages of racial identity in processes that are not linear. Moreover, children in distinct familial and geographical contexts will experience and manifest different responses to their racial environment. These may correlate with various stages of racial identity development but do not necessarily nor strictly pertain to age. Having said that, it is the case that earlier chapters in this book do tend to offer strategies that make more sense with younger children, while later chapters address issues more likely to emerge among older kids.

The chapters are organized thematically. Chapter 1 starts us off by exploring the basic differences between color-blind and race-conscious parenting. From there we'll engage one of the first questions parents tend to ask: where do I start (chapter 2)? Then, after discussing the basic question of what a healthy white racial identity looks like (chapter 3), the remaining chapters each take up common and particular questions that emerge in parenting white children.

In the last several years, I have spent countless hours working with white people on how to become strong allies and advocates for racial justice; especially in the current national racial crisis that is impacting us all. Time and time again, parents have asked me how the theories and tools I have offered for adults in those spaces might translate to parenting practices—especially with younger children who are developmentally not yet able to talk about race and racism in the ways older youth might be able to.

It was a result of working with these parents and resonating with their questions as a parent myself that I decided to write *Raising White Kids*. More important, it was as a result of taking these parents' questions seriously that I have written it to be practical, concrete, and constructive. In every chapter, parents and other caregivers will find examples of what implementing race-conscious engagement of children looks like. It's my hope adults can take these examples, and what they learn from them, and envision age-appropriate, context-specific practices with the children in their lives.

But here's the most important thing you need to know to get started: another world is possible. We have the capacity to transform this racial crisis. To transform it we must have both the will and a different set of tools and frameworks than those that got us to this point. *Raising White Kids* offers one important set of tools. I will say it again. Know this: we have a long way to go, but *we can go.*

Takeaways

✓ We live in a society that is racially unjust, that is deeply segregated, and that privileges our (white) racial group. But we *can* teach our kids a commitment to equity and social justice.

✓ We know that teaching children to be color-blind or to value diversity is an inadequate strategy.

✓ Racial development is no different than physical, intellectual, or emotional development.

✓ Race-conscious parenting means talking about race—and racism—early and often in our children's lives.

✓ Developing antiracism in our kids, and living it ourselves, is a central commitment in what it means to raise healthy white children in a racially unjust America.

CHAPTER 1

From Color-Blindness to Race-Conscious Parenting

"I've always taught my children to treat everyone with kindness and fairness no matter who they are or what their circumstances and my kids do have friends of a lot of different races and from different cultures. They never seemed to notice or care what race someone was, until they came home from school after Martin Luther King Jr. Day last year. Then, all of a sudden, they were talking about people's race all the time, saying things like 'Our friend Joe...he's Black, right?' And I felt like they actually might have been better off without that celebration. Because I really don't think it's good for them to focus on people's race and put them in boxes! Isn't that the opposite of what we should be trying to do?"

The concern this mother is expressing is not an uncommon one among white parents. Her suspicion about the move in school to emphasize difference comes from her sense that a color-blind approach might better support harmonious relationships among racially diverse children than an approach that emphasizes their differences and seems to put them in boxes—or even makes them start to put one another in boxes. This mother is not expressing resistance to difference, itself. Quite the contrary, she seems to value it. But she's afraid that teaching children to notice and name racial difference is backfiring. She wants her children to recognize human dignity, value equality, and embrace everyone. Rightly so!

Color-blindness became one of the most prominent ways to approach race and difference in the United States after the civil rights movement. The basic principles of color-blindness include the idea that we shouldn't notice race, should look past race, and/or, especially, should never use race as the basis for making decisions, policies, or judgments about people.

Such principles can obviously be used in a cynical way. Color-blindness can be used, for example, to shut down racial discussions before they even get started—that is, "We're all just human after all, so why don't we just get over it?"

Color-blindness can also be used to short-circuit attempts to respond to the long-term effects of racism. Namely, decade upon decade of racist policies and practices have created uneven playing fields. If we want to address such unevenness in the interest of creating equity, we have no choice but to notice race. We have to use it in some way to develop policies and practices aimed at leveling the playing field. Granted, there are legitimate discussions to be had in response to difficult questions and diverse perspectives on how we best do that. But if color-blindness is invoked at the start of such inquiry, any serious discussion about how to even out the field is shut down before it can even begin.

The motivations behind color-blindness are often genuine and full of good intentions, however, as is true in the case of this mother. Indeed, color-blindness is an outgrowth of a central moral message of the civil rights movement: we're one human family and race should never cause a difference in treatment. Many of us have rightly learned, moreover, that assuming someone's race can tell you anything meaningful about that person is the epitome of racial stereotyping. So the conclusion that a good way to teach our children tolerance and equality is to teach them to not notice or to look past race is actually really logical. Color-blindness seems to stand on sound moral reasoning.

> Color-blindness doesn't work for the simple reason that we cannot *not* see race.

To top it all off, there is at least one more reason color-blindness can be so appealing. Many serious challenges do emerge when we start to name and notice race. This is especially the case as we teach children to do so. What does it mean to say Joe is "Black"? Does Joe identify that way? What are these children assuming they know about Joe or saying about him by debating whether or not he is Black? Obviously, it's a problem if white children run around loudly labeling other children, and especially if they do so in ways that don't feel good or accurate to those children so labeled.

Later in this book we'll return and dig in to these challenges and explore ways race-conscious parenting helps with them. At this point it's important to simply be clear: to "not see" or "not name" race is not a solution to the challenges this mother raises. So let's begin by understanding why color-blindness fails if the goal is to teach white children to value everyone and work for equity and justice, and why, in fact, color-blindness actually causes harm to white children's understanding of race. After that we'll explore some of the reasons teaching our children to value diversity as a primary parental strategy, although better, also falls short and what race-conscious parenting looks like in contrast to these two approaches.

Color-Blindness Doesn't Work

Even when the motivations are good, there are many reasons to reject color-blind approaches in our parenting. First, and most fundamentally, color-blindness doesn't work for the simple reason that we cannot *not* see race. In a society as thoroughly racialized as the United States, unless one has a visual impairment it is literally impossible for any human, past their first few months of life, to "not see" it.

Race is a social construction. This means that differences such as skin tone, hair texture, shapes of faces, and so on don't have any significance or meaning in and of themselves. None of these have any innate bearing on character traits. There is no racial DNA. Instead, such physical attributes are *given* meaning by society through a whole array of social practices.

Before going any further, let me emphasize a very important point. Even though it has no innate meaning, because race *is* given meaning—it has been and continues to be constructed—it *is* real. Sometimes realizing race is not biological leads people to conclude that race is only an illusion. Couldn't we get rid of some of the challenges it creates by just ignoring it?

But constructed realities are real and cannot be ignored. My house is constructed. Just because it was built at some point doesn't mean it doesn't exist. In fact, every time it rains I am especially aware that my house exists and am grateful it does. Further, my house could be remodeled, changed in some fundamental way, or differently constructed. And all of these descriptions of my house are analogous to race as well. (In fact, the understanding that a construction is something that has been built by people is a really helpful part of this analogy when thinking about raising white children. Parents, teachers, and other caregivers are part of the construction crew for children's embodiment of race.)

Because race is social and human beings are deeply social creatures, we learn to see race in and on the bodies of ourselves and others. We also observe, internalize, and eventually mimic the many social practices that abound in daily life that give the physical attributes society uses to "mark" race powerful social meanings and effects. In the United States, the attributes revolve heavily around skin color, but can also be hair, an accent, the sound of a name, and many other overt and subtle markers. This entire process gets underway very early in life—much earlier than many adults presume is possible.

There are thick socialization processes through which we learn to see and feel race. This means race's impact is much

27

deeper and more encompassing than something having only to do with how we think about difference, each other, or with what we believe about people. In other words, race goes beyond just our minds. The ways people of different racial groups speak to one another, hold our bodies as we do so, are or are not present or represented in various physical spaces (especially in a deeply segregated nation)—all of these are dimensions of our social, racial experiences. Imagine how different the space of a predominantly white church, a historically Black church, or a church made of up Latino/a citizens or recent immigrants from Mexico feels when one enters each of these respective spaces, for example. Even as one can imagine the different feels of such distinct spaces, parents need to understand that young children pick up on and experience these differences no less than do adults.

Within a few months of being born, babies begin to observe and absorb, and even respond to the racial dimensions of our society. Children continue to do so throughout their development, day in and day out. This is true whether they are raised in very multicultural contexts or in the whitest of spaces.

Many studies help us understand how early these observations begin. Some studies have provided evidence that by the age of six months babies begin to notice the physical differences that mark race. A chapter in the book *NurtureShock: New Thinking About Children* reports on a number of these studies. It shares one in which, when shown pictures of different faces, babies pause. Their eyes linger longer on pictures in which the face has a different skin tone than that of their parents.[1] Other studies suggest this phenomenon starts as early as three months.[2] Researchers interpret the pause as indicating that babies are noticing skin tone difference—because they don't similarly pause on faces of those who are not their parents but who share the same skin tone as their parents.

Such studies don't mean we are all innately predisposed to racial prejudice. Noticing differences and developing prejudice are two distinct processes. Prejudice is learned. Prejudice is the step taken after one notices physical differences in which differences are assigned meanings—negative ones. One does not inevitably have to take such a step. Rather, the *NurtureShock* studies show that "children's brains are noticing skin color differences and trying to understand their meaning."[3] It's safe to say prejudice is a likely developmental outcome, however. Children neurologically predisposed to notice the physical attributes marking race are immersed in a myriad of social experiences in which people who have such attributes are constantly treated or portrayed in particular ways.

> As early as age five, children recognize that different groups are treated differently.

The point here is to make clear that noticing racial differences is simply part of neurological development. For our purposes, studies like these offer insight into a concrete biological reason color-blind approaches are a nonstarter if we want to raise white children able to engage race, navigate racially diverse environments, and grow deep antiracist sensibilities and abilities. Color-blindness cannot teach children equity because it does not line up with how their brains actually function. They notice racial differences, and if we don't interpret the meaning of these differences with and for them, society will.

Because color-blindness is out of alignment with neural development, it would fail even if the United States had no history of being racially hierarchical or white-dominated and was not replete with legacies of hostility and tensions among racial groups. But we *do* live in a society with such histories, hierarchy, hostilities, and tensions. Encounters among and between people of different racial groups are almost always marked with these tensions, even in amiable contexts. So beside the fact that their brains notice differences, in this act of "neurological noticing" children also take in many nuanced dimensions of tension and racial embodiment that constantly impact interracial exchanges in our society, however subtle these may seem to adults.

Many other studies have demonstrated that the youngest of children internalize racist perceptions of themselves and of others.[4] As early as age five, children recognize that different groups are treated differently. They understand something about the social status of different racial groups—their own group and others'.[5]

It's pretty remarkable how astute children are and the precision with which they interpret the social meanings of race. Other types of studies have shown that the youngest of children begin to "play" with race as they engage one another.

Sociologists Debra Van Ausdale and Joe R. Feagin conducted a yearlong, in-depth study of a multicultural preschool. Van Ausdale spent countless hours observing children's interactions with one another. In *The First R: How Children Learn Race and Racism*, Van Ausdale transcribes story after story in which children as young as three or four, themselves of many different racial and ethnic identities, make both subtle and overt references to race and difference as they play with one another.

The children Van Ausdale observed enacted larger social messages in sophisticated ways. Many of these messages adults might assume would go right over their heads. To share just one account, Van Ausdale transcribes an exchange among two white girls (both aged four) and one Asian girl (age three) who are playing with a wagon. One of the white girls is pulling the other two children. When the wagon gets stuck the Asian girl jumps out to help pull. The white girl responds,

> "No, no. You can't pull this wagon. Only white
> Americans can pull this wagon." Renee has her hands
> on her hips and frowns at Lingmai. The Asian girl tries
> again to lift the handle of the wagon, and Renee again
> insists that only "white Americans" are permitted to do
> this task.[6]

Here, a four-year-old is using a construction that joins race and perceptions of citizenship to exclude in her play. This is complex understanding on display. She already knows something about the white racial assumptions of who counts as American.

I frequently hear adults who see or hear of children acting

in ways that look like bigotry simply conclude: "Well, obviously, they must've been taught this at home!" This is a tempting explanation. Shocked to hear an exchange like the one between Renee and Lingmai, it seems clear an adult must have said something direct for such a young child to invoke such a blatantly racist trope. Children, we believe, are so innocent.

But there are many reasons to reject this one-dimensional explanation. Most important, it leads us to conclude that if we aren't actively teaching racial bigotry at home, then our own kids won't fall prey to mimicking such messaging. This conclusion couldn't be further from the truth. If we believe overtly bigoted parenting is the only or even main cause of the kind of behavior seen in the wagon incident, we don't appreciate how pervasive racial messages are and how deeply observant our children are. These messages are everywhere and our children take it all in.

Let me share an example from the world of gender. When my oldest daughter was four, she told me one day that she knew "God must be a boy." Now, I'm not only a feminist, but I have training in theology. I have many great arguments about why giving God a gender—especially a male gender—is not only *not sound theology*, but actually reinforces sexism. My feminist Christian self was beyond alarmed.

But the declaration got worse. When I began to probe and ask how she knew God was a boy, first she said something about "God" being obviously a boy's name. But then she said, "God has to be a boy, because boys are better than girls!"

An outsider listening in, someone who knew nothing about

my children or me, might understandably assume that such a confident declaration must have been taught in our home. What four-year-old would otherwise spout such sexist non-sense? But such a conclusion wouldn't be more off base. My kids are being raised by two moms. Both of us buck many of the common stereotypes about gender. Neither of us has con-sciously given either of our children anything but intentionally positive messages about both gender equity and fluidity. We are overtly pro-girl and antisexist in our modeling and teaching.

But gender and gender messages are everywhere. So are race and racial messages. "Generally speaking, whites and people of color do not occupy the same social space or social status, and this very visible fact of American life does not go unnoticed by children," for example.[7] This and so many other realities of racial life in the United States are absorbed by our children who go on to make conclusions about them—con-clusions such as this: *If white Americans are at the top of our racial hierarchy, pointing out Lingmai's difference from me on this front is an effective way to make sure I get to keep control of the wagon!*

The preschool where the wagon incident took place had an explicitly multicultural mission and curriculum. That doesn't mean no racist teaching was taking place in any of the homes of the children who attended the school. But one could reason-ably conclude that many or most families sending their children to such a school weren't explicitly engaging in such teaching. As is true with sexism and many other "isms," the reality is the presence of racial messaging and experiences is pervasive and powerful. These transpire and impact our children well outside of specific parental language and teachings.

Children observe the world around them so carefully. They notice patterns. For example, they see how many places and spaces have only one racial group present in them (and which racial groups are present in what kinds of places). They notice who holds which jobs at supermarkets, restaurants, schools, or doctors' offices. They then generalize what they see to draw specific (false) conclusions about why it would be that doctors are white and custodians are Latino/a, or why no Black people go to church, and on and on. If children aren't taught the causes of the inequity they see, explains antiracism activist Emma Redden, their observations combined with the racist messages they pick up from various forms of media lead "them to assume then that inequality is a reflection of people's intelligence, capability, or skills." Meanwhile, Redden writes, "talking about racism is not actually 'telling them about something they didn't even know existed,' but helping them understand what they witness, experience and/or participate in every day."[8] Direct adult intervention is necessary, then, to challenge and question the conclusions children will otherwise draw, conclusions that will reflect the broader, racist messages that float freely throughout society. We can't intervene if we're teaching color-blindness.

As psychologist Beverly Daniel Tatum, an expert in racial identity development, puts it, racism is like smog in the air.[9] We all breathe it in, every day. Our children inhale it from the moment they are born. The examples I've just shared from careful sociological and psychological studies could not make the truth of Tatum's claim any clearer. If it's literally the case that we cannot *not see* race because of our neurological wiring—and if children are absorbing negative messages about racial differences from the moment they draw breath—but we avoid talking explicitly about differences, then we are deluding ourselves about what the results will be. We fail to equip our children for the long-term in a fundamentally important way.

As we abdicate the responsibility of specific, clear racial teaching in our children's lives, we step away from them at the precise point we need to be intentionally stepping in. Without us, society's deeply racist messaging and the profound racial tensions that permeate life in the United States move in and take over. Our children continue to develop and interpret race's meanings, whether or not we actively cultivate this development. Even when they are rooted in good intentions, color-blind parental approaches leave our children on their own to just keep breathing in society's "smog" without benefit of a face mask. And the impact is serious: left untended, racialized behaviors and perceptions of self and others that are innocent at age three will not remain innocent by age ten, twelve, or twenty.

There's another reason to reject color-blindness. Even if we could actually choose to not see race, being unable to see race renders us unable to see and address racism. If my children's ability to challenge and resist racism when they encounter it is important, then I must utterly and actively reject color-blindness. Over the long-term, the only way to address and challenge racism is to practice and learn effective strategies for doing so.

Generic teachings like "we're all equal" don't counteract racism.

There are two other kickers worth sharing at this point. During her year spent at the preschool, Van Ausdale discovered that the same children playing with race also already knew that adults considered such behavior inappropriate. Thus they would often hide their racialized play. When the conflict came to a head in the wagon episode, for example, what was reported to the teacher was simply that the four-year-old girl was "being mean." In numerous other scenarios kids similarly downplayed or evaded the racial nature of the meanness that had resulted in a conflict. "Children were usually encouraged to be 'friends' and to 'work out' their difficulties without name-calling and anger, but [racial] details of their conflicts were rarely offered to teachers, nor did the teachers seem to expect such particulars."[10]

This doesn't surprise me. Children pick up on taboos very easily and know when they are violating them. Just one incident managed to convey to me that something was very wrong with what J. had said to me. The power of taboos around race make it all the more urgent that parents and teachers step in and give children language, tools, and support to navigate the difficult social life in which the United States places all children.

The second kicker is more counterintuitive. Teachings such as "we're all the same inside" or "we're all equal" do not serve our children any better than does silence. To this point, one might want to respond to everything I've said with, "But I want my children to value everyone, of all races," or "I want to be sure my children understand that we are all human." In fact, when the mother in my opening example said she was worried celebrating Martin Luther King Jr. Day had caused her kids to notice race in ways they shouldn't, and that she wanted her kids to treat everyone with kindness, this is precisely what she was calling for. To all of these desires, I would first respond, "Yes! I want that for my children too."

But numerous studies also make clear that generic teachings like "we're all equal" don't counteract racism. One reason is that such teachings are much too vague for young children to understand. When parents teach "we're all friends," as a way to talk about valuing everyone regardless of differences, children have no idea they're supposed to connect that teaching to skin color.[11] Researcher Po Bronson writes about a friend who "repeatedly told her five-year-old son, 'Remember, everybody's equal.' She thought she was getting the message across. Finally, after seven months of this, her boy asked, 'Mommy, what's "equal" mean?'"[12]

Equality is an important aspiration. It is a value many of us long to implement. But it is a very abstract notion. When it's used as a way to teach race it becomes an empty mantra. As I often say to my college students, "Yes, we're all human, at our core. But have you ever met another human who had no race, no gender, no sex, no class, and so on?" They always answer no. "That's right," I respond, "the only way we show that we *actually* respect our shared humanity, is by taking people's specific, diverse experiences of their humanity very seriously."

We've got to do the same with our kids. If we want children who value everyone, and who deeply and authentically understand we're all part of shared humanity, if we want them to actually live in ways that help to realize equity, the only route is to consciously and explicitly teach them about difference!

Color-Blindness Causes Harm

I hope it is clear by this point why color-blindness fails as a parenting strategy. Before moving on, I want to take the case against color-blindness one step further. Color-blindness doesn't simply not work, it is actually harmful to our children. It damages their ability to embrace equity.

Color-blind teaching presents as an aspiration ("don't see it!") a charge that is fundamentally out of synch with their daily experience ("I see it everywhere!"). In doing so, it actively distorts children's engagement with and interpretation of reality. When we teach an approach to race that fundamentally clashes with children's actual experiences and emerging knowledge, we are active participants in this distortion.

Imagine the long-term impact if a parent or teacher repeatedly insisted to a child that he should call the sky green, as the child is meanwhile learning his colors, pointing at the sky, and saying blue! "No," says the caregiver, "that's green." It's not difficult to imagine the intellectual distortion and confusion that would emerge out of such a contradictory toggle between the child's experience and adult response. Neither is it difficult to imagine the emotional distortion that would result from such disorienting messaging being repeatedly conveyed by someone the child trusts.

The cognitive dissonance of color-blindness cannot help but disable our children's attempts to put their experiences into meaningful language and develop concepts that resonate with something resembling reality. On its own, this dissonance is damaging. But the consequences to the parent-child relationship are also serious. Over time, meaningful parent-child dialogue on an aspect of social experience in which this contradictory set of teachings is being experienced is extinguished. The possibility of needed mentorship and nurture in regard to race becomes deeply eroded because the child knows his or her parent is not being truthful.

A second harm of color-blind teaching comes in regard to the impact of white children's relationships with children of color. The children in the opening example may or may not have handled their discussion of Joe's racial identity appropriately. But if these kids are friends with Joe and Joe is, indeed, Black, it's unlikely they'll be able to sustain a meaningful friendship with him for the long haul if this mother goes with her gut and insists on countering their school teaching with color-blind messaging.

Race and racism matter in the lives of children of color, and they are recognized by such children as mattering, in deep and profound ways. This recognition happens early. On top of that, we know parents of such children, at rates two to five times more often than their white counterparts, teach their children explicitly and in age-appropriate ways about the many ways race matters in their lives.[13]

As children of color develop and learn the ways race matters while white children are left alone to internalize racism or taught to actively ignore race, the possibility of meaningful friendships and connections between children of different races becomes more remote. Many observers have noted that elementary-age children in racially diverse settings play contentedly across racial lines. By middle school these same children start to self-segregate.[14] Interracial friendships among adolescents are exceedingly rare. If you account for all other variables (for example, different demographics in a school setting), youth are almost twice as likely to form a same-race friendship than an interracial one.[15]

There are many reasons for these dynamics. For example, adolescents go through all kinds of new, personal self-identity explorations that impact interracial friendships. Many teenagers, of various racial identities, begin to explore their individual relationship with their "own" racial group.[16] And the racial dynamics that exist in many school environments (between teachers and administrators, and students) in the United States have an effect on kids' friendships, as well.[17] But aside from all of this, it also stands to reason that if white children become increasingly unable to identify with, to understand, or even begin to actively deny what becomes for children of color a deep and formative dimension of daily life experience, authentic meaningful friendships across racial lines would be very difficult.

In fact, the difficulty of cross-racial friendships—a near impossibility if the white partner in the friendship doesn't understand race—is one reason teaching children to value diversity or even making sure white children experience diverse contexts as they grow *does not solve the problem* of how to raise white kids. There are serious benefits to experiencing diversity early in life for raising antiracist white children. But if parents don't take up discussions of race and racism explicitly with children, they are unlikely to succeed in remaining good friends to children of color over time.

A third harm of color-blindness is most directly antithetical to the goal of raising healthy white children. There is an often-unspoken but fundamental message on which color-blindness rests—whether we realize it or not—that there is something wrong with color.

> Race-conscious parenting is a broad and proactive way of thinking about how we engage race with our children.

Consider the moments in which white children are taught to not notice race. These are almost always moments in which a white child hears that it's not good to notice the race of a person of color. It is rare-to-never that children are told not to notice someone is white. White is typically not marked in the same way that being Black or Latino/a is marked. Thus a message intended to communicate that "all races are as good as each other, don't notice" is actually received by kids as "it doesn't matter that that person is Black or Latino/a, we should like that person *anyway*." The implication is that blackness or brownness is somehow undesirable or shameful. It shouldn't be held against the person. And, more subtly, we white people are somehow doing well and being kind by not noticing that difference.

Race matters everywhere one turns in our society. Thus, color-blindness can only mislead and present children with a false view of reality. Even if it is used as an aspirational message, color-blind teachings backfire badly. They convey to children that something is wrong with people of color, ask them to ignore their own observations, and fail to support them in developing language for their own experiences, thus actively impeding a crucial area of their moral and social development.

What is Race-Conscious Parenting?

Race-conscious parenting is an approach that insists on noticing and naming race early and often. Being race conscious means thinking about, talking about, acting in response to the recognition (or consciousness) of race. It means noticing race, seeing race, and admitting that we do so in direct and overt ways. This approach stands in dramatic and stark contrast to color-blindness.

Race-conscious parenting is a broad and proactive way of thinking about how we engage race with our children, and teach and live out antiracist commitments with them on a regular, day-to-day basis. This broad approach rests on particular understandings about what race is, and how it is communicated and experienced that will be taken up throughout this entire book. But in addition to this big picture, race-conscious parenting also enables particular responses and postures in the many specific, challenging racial moments parents in the United States so often face.

To make this concrete right away, I'd like to illustrate the contrast between the behaviors to which a color-blind response versus a race-conscious response lead. Let's take two examples many parents of white children will recognize; the first is hypothetical, the second is an actual experience I had with my daughter.

> *Example 1: A parent is out grocery shopping with his three-year-old. His white child sees an African American person in the same aisle. She points and says, "Look at that woman's brown skin." The embarrassed father quickly shushes the child and whisks her away from the encounter.*

> *Example 2: One day at school my six-year-old pointed at a Black student who looked to be a couple of years older than she, who was standing at her locker putting away her backpack. "Look," she pointed, "that kid looks like A. [my daughter's cousin, who also happens to be Black]!" I froze.*

Can you imagine yourself in either of these scenarios? Just as in the case of Ms. B. and two six-year-olds outside a bathroom talking about starting a white club, few parents of white children can fail to appreciate how much anxiety either of these scenes would evoke. The anxiety here is not triggered by the pointing alone. Children do rude things all the time and, as parents, we know it's simply part of our job to teach them otherwise. The anxiety has everything to do with the racial dimension of these encounters.

But even though they are understandable given the anxiety evoked by each situation, the shushing and whisking in the grocery store causes a huge problem. These are enacted versions of "be color-blind" or "don't notice!" It's not difficult to see how shushing and whisking this child away, especially if this parent fails to have a follow-up conversation that specifically addresses the racial dimensions of this exchange, will almost surely be understood by the child as noticing race is bad. Even telling this child generically "it's rude to point" won't cut it in terms of interrupting that conclusion.

More alarming, the child is likely to infer there's something wrong with racial difference itself and with blackness specifically. (Again, it's unlikely a white child is ever going to point like this at a white person, so she's not going to get messages that there's something wrong with white.) This learning that something is wrong with blackness may be so subtle it's indiscernible at first. And it might not happen in just this one moment of encounter. But over time, when coupled with more overt teachings of color-blindness, it will become very powerful.

Of course, the solution here is obviously not to allow this young child to continue to point at people of color! But at this point, a race-conscious parental approach offers a really different set of assumptions, asks a different set of questions, and moves toward different kinds of reactions than a color-blind approach.

First, we have already rejected the notion that children should not notice or observe race—even if they could do so. So even while we need to support them in growing their abilities to discuss race aloud, we do not assume a three-year-old should not have made this remark. Instead, the starting assumption is that *what this three-year-old did was a developmentally normal activity*. Our task as a parent, then, is both to support our child in engaging in a more appropriate manner but to do so while simultaneously affirming and encouraging the fact that she is noticing race and giving her a positive description of difference.

In short, the noticing itself needs to be affirmed, supported—even celebrated! The awkward and inappropriate—but utterly age-appropriate—parts of this scene need to be redirected.

So what could that look like in this uncomfortable moment? Well, a race-conscious parental response to the grocery store encounter is going to consider first whether the woman saw and heard the child. If she did, minimally, a response to the child within earshot of the woman is appropriate and necessary. This response might go something like this, "Honey, it's not polite to point at people. But, yes, that woman's skin is a beautiful shade of brown." Depending on the situation, a turn to directly address the adult who has been pointed at might be appropriate as well.

Right off the bat this response takes the child and her developmental state seriously. It responds without further loading the moment just because it happens to be about race. Race is loaded for both adults in this scenario but is not, yet, for this three-year-old. This response treats this moment no differently than it would treat other moments of pointing (namely, pointing is rude).

This response also treats the woman being pointed at with the respect she deserves. That is treatment the white tendency to avert the eyes and rush away from uncomfortable situations simply does not offer. Besides giving this woman her due, such a response also models for the child a critical nonverbal teaching: direct engagement of other people if, or when, we have been disrespectful (even unintentionally) is no less appropriate in racially fraught situations than it is in any other situation. The proposed response I describe here is the equivalent of making a child who forgets to say thank you go back and do so.

There is no doubt an encounter like this remains awkward. It may or may not bother the person at whom your child has pointed. You may not ever even know. Everyone is different. The best we can do as a parent in this moment is to know and accept that and to assume that our public and visible attempt— because the pointing was public and visible—to positively characterize dark skin and teach our child about the importance of being polite to others is required. This remains the case whether or not the woman was bothered.

It's worth noting that when we as adults commit to daily living out our belief that we should notice race and teach our children to do so, we become better equipped to respond well in challenging situations. Part of the discomfort of this situation is that white adults tend to have little daily practice in talking about and responding to race; race feels loaded for us because we don't engage it directly as often as we should. When we do so with regularity, even if they remain awkward, moments like these cause much less anxiety. Racial tensions and challenges are real because we are all impacted, and our relationships are all impacted, by the racially fraught context in which we live. But the more we engage, the more we develop emotional intelligence and resiliency for navigating the many racial tensions and challenges that exist in our worlds.

A second point is worth noting here as well. Early and consistent race-conscious parenting practice actually makes situations like this less likely to happen in the first place. For example, a three-year-old who already has lots of diversity in her life, diversity cultivated in intentional ways (despite the reality that the organization of US society leaves us so racially segregated) is much less likely to point in the grocery store in the first place. Of course, white Americans' social networks are 91 percent composed of white people. So cultivating diversity in our children's lives takes intentional and sustained effort.[18] There's nothing easy about accomplishing actual diversity in segregated America. Nonetheless, white children for whom diversity is more normal are better set up from early on.

The potential of these two gains alone—namely, a reduction in adult anxiety and children less likely to be surprised by difference—is a case for pursuing race-conscious parenting.

But there's an additional gain here, one that might be more unexpected. The more equipped we are as parents, because we ourselves talk about and engage race in our own lives, the less likely we are to impose adult anxiety onto our children. The less we impose anxiety on our children, the greater the likelihood that our responses to them will invite and open up conversations with them, rather than closing them down. And when that happens, sometimes we're going to be happily surprised to find ourselves learning things from our kids or having conversations with them we wouldn't have anticipated. To put it differently, it's been my experience that when I've managed my own anxiety and been therefore able to respond more openly, I often discover some of my anxiety was unfounded to begin with.

Remember? First I froze as I heard my own child (example two, above) seem to enact the worst version of "white child points at and speaks about a black or brown person." Even worse in this scenario, I heard her seem to (loudly) prove the stereotype that white people think all Black people look alike. After I froze I tried consciously to relax and take a deep breath.

"Really?" I said to my daughter (not sure if the other student heard her or not). "In what way does that girl look like A.?" "Her hair!" my daughter responded. "Her hair is just like A.'s hair." And, indeed, it was similar. The girl had dreadlocks; dreadlocks that looked much like cousin A.'s dreadlocks.

"You're right!" I said. "Her hair looks a lot like A.'s. But remember honey, it's not nice to point."

Was my response a perfect response? No. Could it have backfired? Yes—in so many ways. My daughter might have doubled down and said, "Her skin is dark like A.'s." The child to whom she was responding might have heard her. And if these things had happened, I would have addressed my daughter directly and also made sure the other child overheard me as I did. I likely would also have said something directly to the other child, such as, "I don't know if my daughter's observation bothered you, but if it did I'm very sorry."

But even with the risks and the imperfections, this response did not leave my daughter with any residual learning that race, blackness, or difference are not to be noticed, let alone that they are somehow bad, embarrassing or shameful. The words *race* or *Black* were never used at all. But this is an example of the kinds of moves one makes if one is committed to race-conscious parenting.

A Quick Word About Diversity

Race-conscious parenting is different than simply teaching our children they should value diversity and difference. It's important I state this clearly. While color-blind teaching remains a prevalent mode for engaging race with white children (especially among parents), an increasingly common approach, especially in educational and religious contexts, is to teach children and youth to value diversity. The difference between valuing diversity and race-conscious parenting is worth laying out here because, like color-blindness, valuing diversity has proven inadequate. It also fails for reasons we can identify. Naming these reasons helps clarify the aims and approaches that, in contrast, are implied by race-conscious parenting.

The notion that we should value diversity rests on the basic premise that differences should be embraced and celebrated. Many parents are committed to this value. We demonstrate this value in different ways, depending on our families and contexts. Some of us talk with our children about how wonderful our differences are. Others of us may seek to put our children in diverse settings early in life. I have heard many parents, including my own, for example, explain they chose public schools for their kids because they wanted their children to learn in diverse contexts.

This posture of valuing diversity is much improved over color-blindness. In fact, this was the kind of approach taken in the preschool about which I have written. Diversity as a framework avowedly "notices difference." This is highly important. But many approaches to diversity are insufficient. These insufficiencies can backfire in ways that leave white youth little more equipped in racial environments than color-blindness leaves them. When they do backfire it causes great harm to the children or youth of color with whom white youth are in relationships or shared educational contexts.

> White people receive benefits, protections, and privilege in systematic ways while children of color do not.

To put it in stark terms: without a carefully cultivated race-conscious approach to being white, valuing diversity doesn't offer *white* children anything positive to claim or hold on to. The things white children might be able to positively claim as unique to *whiteness* come out of privilege and injustice—so I'm not talking about encouraging kids to hold on to these things!

The challenge of living in a white racial hierarchy, as

opposed to just a diverse society, is that we are not all just *different*. If we lived in a diverse society that was equal and fair in terms of racial treatment, valuing difference would be sufficient. Saying we're all "just different, let's celebrate" would be great. But we live in a society in which white people receive benefits, protections, and privilege in systematic ways while children of color do not. This distinction creates a number of challenges that are unique and specific to parenting white children.

For example, the racial identity white children develop is distinct from that of nonwhite children. If we know that children have internalized racist perceptions of themselves and of others by age five, this means children of color are aware of and have perhaps accepted to some degree negative assessments of their own race. It also means white children are aware of and perhaps have already started to believe there is something superior about themselves as white.[19] The messages children receive in society are different among these different children. Differently raced children thus need different parental responses in search of cultivating their abilities to live lives committed to equity and justice.

What we need to teach white children is complicated. Consider this example by thinking about the phrase "Black is beautiful!" When I ask my college students what they would think if they saw a group of African American students walking across campus carrying signs that said this, they overwhelmingly indicate they would be at least curious and probably supportive. In dramatic contrast the phrase "White is beautiful!" immediately evokes from them a radically different reaction. A

51

group of white students carrying such a sign evokes a fear of white supremacy.

The point of this example is not that it should be okay for white students to carry "White is beautiful" signs. My students are nervous about this for good reason! The point is that the dramatic contrast in these seemingly parallel accounts exposes the limits of teaching our kids to value diversity. Teaching kids to value diversity, on its own, doesn't capture the whole truth about our racial, social life. It doesn't include attention to the fact that white racial domination is the norm in our society. It certainly doesn't equip us to challenge that norm. When we present valuing diversity as the primary or only response to difference, then, we still set white children up for failure.

Being white and committed to equality is complicated in a racial hierarchy. Adults in significant caregiving relationships with kids must figure out how to help them understand and navigate this difficult juxtaposition.

Another way in which diversity fails to offer parents and white children what we need in order to journey toward racial health is a direct outgrowth of this dilemma. When we talk about valuing diversity we are often thinking about learning from our different histories and cultures. But if one is committed to truthfully talking about history and culture, this posture does not go very far in terms of the white racial experience. For example, children of color have freedom fighters we can point to and teach about when the agenda is diversity. If you ask children of color about their culture they usually have something to share and discuss. But the reality of *white* racial history is that white people do not really have "white" histories we can celebrate. Ask any white US American (who is not committed to white supremacy) to talk about white culture and we stumble. White cannot be celebrated in the same way Black or Latino/a can. Our work to value diversity does not admit and wrestle with this problem. But white children experience this problem as they grow (we'll look more closely at how this plays out in older kids in chapter 6).

If we do not explicitly work with white children and youth to understand how they fit in to diversity frameworks, with specific attention to their identity as white people, they are vulnerable to becoming deeply disaffected from and disengaged with diversity. In fact, it may be counterintuitive, but the more diverse the context and the more pronounced the emphasis on diversity, the more disaffected white kids may become, as they lack support for navigating their white social position.

This specific problem, along with responses for it, will be explored in detail later in this book. Here it suffices to be clear that diversity is leaps and bounds better than color-blindness. But if it is not utilized in a manner that enables white youth to find a positive route through which they, as *whites*, can authentically connect or contribute to diversity and to building a just racial present and future, it is not enough.

Race-Conscious Parenting, Some Basic Principles

Race-conscious parenting rests on a number of principles. It goes beyond naming difference and engages with children about the ways difference impacts our experiences.

Race-conscious parenting goes deeper than a commitment to introducing different-colored dolls and toys, reading books at early developmental stages in which diversity is reflected, or participating in multicultural playgroups and schooling. Race-conscious parenting certainly affirms and includes these strategies. But such parenting involves parents (and teachers) seeking out—sometimes even creating—opportunities to address not just race and difference but also racism—proactively and on a regular basis. It also distinctly shapes the kinds of responses adults might make when race and racism are "in the room" in situations that were unanticipated. It actively models and teaches the importance of work against racism and for racial justice.

By explicitly engaging the racial dimensions of experiences, spaces and places, and relationships, and by addressing these in age-appropriate ways, race-conscious parenting conducts a deep reading of the *actual* racial environment. It is able therefore to respond to children's actual experiences, not the racial experiences we wish they were having. It also teaches children as they develop and grow to be able to do the same.

Consider this example. As noted above, many Black children are taught by their parents that they must behave in certain ways around police officers—that is a much more complex discourse than "police officers are safe." If my white daughter is only taught that police are safe, her relationship with her Black cousin, who is (necessarily) being taught that police are complicated, is directly and negatively impacted. The depth and authenticity of that relationship will erode over time. Moreover, her actual racial experience—one in which she will pick up on the many social cues that reveal the truth that police are much more dangerous to some people than others—is ignored.

In contrast, a race-conscious approach assumes my white daughter needs to and *can* be taught about this dimension of the experience of African Americans. She must learn, just as does her cousin, about the complexities of police–civilian relationships. Such learning is critical in support of her ability to develop deep and sustaining individual interracial relationships both in her present and in her future. It also starts her early in the long, complex learning she needs to be able to locate herself in US social structures as a white person. And it builds her own capacity for acting with agency as an advocate for a just, egalitarian, and genuinely diverse society.

Assuming my white eight-year-old needs to have some version of "the talk" (tailored to her specific experience) as does a Black eight-year-old obviously takes us well beyond an approach to race that ends with "embrace and celebrate your cousin's blackness as just as beautiful as your whiteness!" I do want my children to celebrate the blackness of their loved ones. But I also want them to know that society, as a whole, does not. And I want my children to learn that their whiteness needs to make them conscious of the work required to be active anti-racist partners with their beloveds in surviving and challenging such realities.

This basic orientation I am describing here, of course, raises many difficult questions. Figuring out when and how to teach a five-year-old about police killings of Black men, for example, is difficult. Subsequent chapters will explore the complexities we face when teaching about injustice. But the reality is that these questions are not new. Parents of children of color have always asked these questions. Nor are these questions unique. It's not easier for a parent of an African American child to have "the talk" than it is for a white parents. Parents of children of color are only better at it because they have long been doing it.

Those of us who are parents of white children are simply further behind. We have yet to directly face the challenges of talking about race and justice with our children and to develop strong parental strategies. We have yet to cultivate a basic tool kit and set of age-appropriate frameworks for addressing the specific ways these same issues play out with children who are white. But knowing that we must and, more important, that we *can* nurture our children's capacity to function in racially complex, tense, and difficult environments is an essential starting point. Committing to such nurture is critical for enabling our children to constructively address and respond to those environments both now and as they develop and grow.

Race-conscious parenting engages in honest dialogue about the inherited experience of being white, as well as the history of whiteness. It is attentive to the developmental needs of white children. This is not a "white people are bad" approach to parenting. Rather, by responding to children's actual environments, race-conscious parenting teaches advocacy and anti-racism combined with the values of equality and justice. Thus, even as white children are parented to take seriously the ways their location in a white racial hierarchy privileges them, it supports their growth into a sensibility that helps them navigate this with antiracist commitment. It models for them the reality that a commitment to equality and justice as a white person is not only viable but deeply empowering.

So these are the basic assumptions. When it comes to parenting white children for racial justice, there are many unanswered questions. There are also many questions in regard to which there are few clear-cut right and wrong answers. Every child is different. Each family is different. But in much of what follows, examples and possibilities, questions and exploratory responses to these questions, will be laid out. My commitment as a guide is to be part of an emerging conversation taking place among parents of white children who are seeking to raise a generation of equity, justice-committed children far more able and equipped than were most of us—despite having been raised by well-intentioned parents—currently reading this book.

Takeaways

✓ Color-blindness *seems* like a good idea, but it doesn't address the unlevel playing field created by generations of racist policies and practices. And the simple fact is, we cannot *not* see race. Race matters everywhere one turns in our society.

✓ The celebration of diversity as a framework avowedly "notices difference." Noticing differences and developing prejudice are two distinct processes: Prejudice is learned. Seeing racial differences is natural neurological development.

✓ Children notice racial differences and pick up on individual and structural racism from young ages.

✓ We need to proactively interpret the meaning of racial differences for our children or they will simply absorb the negative messages about race and people of color that pervade our society. Telling children to not notice race or that race doesn't matter actively distorts their interpretation of reality.

✓ Children need concrete language about racial justice and antiracism because messages like "we're all equal" are too abstract for them.

✓ Race-conscious parenting is an approach that insists on noticing and naming race early and often. Talking authentically about race and racism responds to children's actual experiences and teaches children as they develop and grow to be able to do the same.

CHAPTER 2

Where Do I Start?

I carried my three-year-old on a carrier on my back, while my five-year-old played on the steps. On the way to the protest I had explained to my children, "An African American teenager was hurt terribly by a white police officer. We're going downtown to be with a whole bunch of people who are sad and angry about it. We want to let the government know we want everyone to be treated fairly and kept safe in this country."

Partway through the protest my five-year-old stopped playing and looked up at me. In a tone imitating a few of the protest's speakers she announced loudly, "Black people aren't safe!" Then she said (just as loudly): "But we're white, so we're safe! Right?"

Thick layers of silence have tended to pervade white communities when it comes to honest, explicit discussions of race. Whether a result of anxiety, awareness of racial tension, or ingrained habits created by the discourse of color-blindness, the long-term effects of silence are powerful. They make it difficult for many white adults to begin to speak about race openly and explicitly. But as with any skill set, we only learn to do it and get better at it, and—in that process—develop even clearer insights into how to do it well through practice. There's simply no way around the awkward, challenging feelings of starting to talk about race. We have to go straight through them by doing it.

> Children begin to work out their racial perceptions, concepts, and ideas long before they can articulate them.

Even if we know the only route is through, it can still be difficult to know where to begin. This chapter is intended to help with that. Exploring examples and comparisons can help us better understand what the principles of race-conscious parenting look like in action. The kinds of examples I use vary, because our children vary in their ages, context, personalities, and on and on. We need lots of stories of trial and error in order to feed our parental imaginations so we can create responses to our own kids.

Most of the examples used to flesh out the "getting started" discussions in this chapter reflect the types of moves and needs that emerge in response to younger children. Still, even as such examples may not pertain precisely to readers whose kids are already a bit older, the why and the how behind various responses shared here align with the goals of cultivating healthy white identity among kids of any age.

It's Never Too Early to Start

Wherever we are in our parenting journey there's a fundamental principle at work in this notion of getting started. It's this: there isn't an age later in our children's lives at which we can suddenly safely begin doing so. There's no moment after which they are suddenly old enough or cognitively ready to discuss race and antiracism. There's not a day at which point it becomes newly appropriate to share with them the more difficult truths about racism, whereas it somehow hadn't been the day before. As with any other development, our children begin to work out their racial perceptions, concepts, and ideas long before they can articulate them verbally or discuss them in an intellectually clear manner. So even while the specific ways we engage will vary from child to child, personality to personality, age to age, the basic principle is that we must start this engagement as soon as we parents are aware there's something to start!

For parents with younger kids, it's worth knowing that if we wait to engage in explicit race talk we may find ourselves engaging, for example, a fifteen-year-old who is still in an early and underdeveloped stage of racial identity (we're going to talk about how racial identity develops in chapter 3). He won't be further along developmentally simply because he's older chronologically. If we wait, our children and youth will have already moved through various racial experiences that will have impacted them. They will have seen people being treated differently because of race, for example, and thus been thrown into cognitive dissonance because they've also been told "we believe in equality" in this country. Without adult interpretive support, they may draw any number of conclusions about why inequity exists that *we wouldn't endorse*. If we wait, our children and youth will have long since internalized racist

> We need to invite conversation and reflection even when we don't have all the answers or quite know how to do it "right."

assumptions and conclusions to some extent—often without even recognizing it.

But even if our child hasn't experienced such dissonance or internalized racism, abruptly letting her in on a truly distressing new learning may well cause her to respond in confusion or frustration, "Why wouldn't you tell me this sooner?" I see this kind of reaction among nineteen-year-olds in my college classes all the time. They are angry no one has told them the truth and feel like they've been living a lie.

However that fifteen-year-old responds, even if she's open to new knowledge and the conversation goes well, she'll still be well behind her peers of color in terms of her facility in antiracist understanding and growth. She'll certainly be well behind where she might have been if we had made different parental choices.

What if your child is already fifteen when you've picked up this book? The way we go about the work described as necessary in this chapter will be different. But the underlying principles are the same. We need to get explicit and be direct about race. We need to invite conversation and reflection even

There is no "too young" in terms of introducing race and racism.

when we don't have all the answers or quite know how to do it "right." This will require us to create opportunities with our kids where race will come up—a protest, watching the news together. We need to be consistently honest about the reality of racial inequity. We need to ask our kids about interracial relationships and racial dynamics at school, make it part of our dialogue with them. Though the how will look different with a teenager, grappling with the principles described in this chapter will help parents of older kids begin to imagine what some specific moves might look like. (And more examples are coming for you later!)

My experience taking my young kids to protest the killing of Michael Brown in Ferguson raises a number of issues. One is the complex question of taking children to protests. Discerning the wisdom (or not) of such a decision is explored later. A second came up when my daughter loudly vocalized a sense of relief that being white made her safe, in a public space where people of color were grieving and protesting their radical lack of safety. I'll return to this part of the experience later in this chapter.

I begin with a third issue this experience raised, which is the central focus of this chapter: there is no "too young" in terms of introducing race and racism. My children were too young to fully understand what was going on at that protest. But I took them nonetheless because I was clear that important development having to do with cultivating their race-conscious schema was taking place in that experience.

Creating a Race-Conscious Schema

Children take in awareness of race and racism long before they have language for it. Adults tend to think of racism as a set of cognitive beliefs or ideas about race. But we often experience race or the presence of racial differences in our bodies. Sometimes we perceive fraught racial dynamics or the presence of racial tensions through body language, speech tones, or even the use of silence, as opposed to particular words being used in a given moment.

The question of where to start, then, begins with our children's deepest assumptions about the world. Our parental work is to knit together, as part of our children's most basic, formative *schema*, a notion of race as visible and normal, an awareness of racial injustice, and a working presumption that people can and do take actions against racism.

Schemas are deep underlying organizational patterns through which we make sense of the world. They are conceptual frameworks. They make up our most fundamental working assumptions about what is normal or true in life—how things simply *are*. When it comes to race, we want the schema through which our children view the world to be one in which race is always visible to them and is just assumed by them to be something we should notice and name. Again, this requires attention to race from the youngest of ages, long before our kids have cognitive capacity to conceptualize racism as an abstract concept.

A race-conscious schema can become the operative schema from where our children begin and through which

65

they look out into and take action in the world. When it does we are already much better poised to naturally support them in developing language for such observations and experiences, and moving along to active antiracist commitments in the world.

But every single day, the society in which we live offers our kids, at best, a color-blind schema and, at worst, a racist one. They are told in many places and in many ways that "we're all the same underneath our skin." They are told that race doesn't really matter. At the same time, they observe and internalize many incidents of racially disparate treatment and negative images and messages about people of color.

Because this happens long before they have words to ask about such things, it's especially critical we take the initiative to talk early and often about race and racism. Doing so is essential for countering the pervasive presence and power of society's constant socialization. As with any powerful collective socializing messages, parents have to go above and beyond what we otherwise would in an environment that was actually race- and difference-neutral or in which antiracism got equal air time to apathetic or racist engagements in the world. But the scales are not balanced. If a child receives messages about color-blindness ten times a day, then the much, much smaller number of people who insist on race-consciousness have to amplify their voices a lot. They need to make sure to insist on race-consciousness at least eleven times a day—each!

What I'm trying to get us to think about here is our role as adult caregivers in proactively helping to form the most deep-seated and taken-for-granted backdrop of assumptions our kids have about what is true and what reality is like. An example by way of analogy can make this clearer.

My children have always known families can have two moms. They won't need to be told this surprising new information when they are suddenly old enough to understand the concept of sexual orientation. This reality has just long been assumed by them—built into their basic schema from the beginning. It shapes the lens through which they see the world. As soon as they experienced "mom," they knew a kid could have two of these. This knowledge was part of their schema before they could even say *mom* or count to the number two.

As our kids got a little older and began to have increased exposure to other families and different family's cultures, their understanding of what makes a family was already on our side. Here's what I mean. At times my kids have experienced social messages or occasional statements by other kids at school that "two girls can't get married" or "you have to have a mom and a dad." But even though such messages are the dominant discourse about families, my kids experienced such beliefs and perceptions as cultural outliers. *These messages are strange and need explanation.* It has never occurred to my kids that they might somehow be the outliers who have to justify the legitimacy of their family. Their schema has long since already assumed two-mom-families as normal. This was (and is) a powerful starting point. From here it will be much easier to support them in navigating the pervasive heterosexism they will encounter in the world as they grow.

Of course, like any children in a heterosexually oriented culture, my kids recognized early—before they had words for it—that their family was less common. They probably even observed negative interpretations of LGBT families early as well. This probably happened in moments that we, their parents, didn't even notice. But we've never had to justify or make a case for two moms. We've simply had to start slowly, in age-appropriate ways, explaining heterosexism to them.

Meanwhile this analogy makes it possible to see something else that pertains directly to cultivating race-conscious schema. It's been easier to knit two-mom-families-are-normal into our kids' schema because they have two. But children being raised by a mom and a dad can also be supported in cultivating a pro-LGBT, pro-diverse families schema as well. Heterosexual parents can (and some do) actively teach their children from early ages that families are all different. They can make sure to constantly disrupt the ideas and images that socialize children early to believe there is only one kind of family (heterosexual) and other kinds of families aren't really legitimate. So even kids who don't have two moms can similarly start from an inclusive norm in regard to which heterosexism is the outlier that eventually needs explanation.

All of this is parallel to what I'm advocating for parents of white kids to work for in intentionally creating race-conscious schemas in and with our young children. Children begin to knit schemas together immediately. They do it all the time and about everything. Their minds are developing rapidly from before the moment of birth. In any area of developmental life left to be formed without active parental engagement, prevailing social messaging and cultural contexts in which our children are developing will form it first.

It becomes obvious, then, why explicit race talk early in our children's lives is critical. Without it they will have long since knit together a schema somewhere on a continuum of colorblind-to-racist simply because they'll have absorbed it from the broader culture. Once they've done that we have a heck of a lot more teaching and dismantling to do when we finally realize we need to step in and teach our white kids how to challenge racism.

In contrast, raising antiracist children on a journey toward healthy white identities is much easier when we've been actively knitting a race-conscious schema with them from the beginning. It proactively shapes their intellectual development and explicitly forms their powers of observation. In addition, we effectively start a running dialogue with them, which helps us to discover and develop age-appropriate language between ourselves as parent and child. Race talk itself—and antiracist commitments and strategies—become simply a normal, necessary part of life.

Talking About Difference Early and Often

I'm sure you've noticed many parents babble at their young kids. Before you had kids this might have even looked really silly to you. Maybe you thought, "I'll never do that when I'm a parent!" Then you became a parent.

We spend hours pointing out and describing the world to our babies, toddlers, and young children. We do it without even noticing we're doing it. We chatter about what our kids are seeing, point out and name the color of sky, ask them the same questions over and over—questions we know the answer to and know they know the answer to ("what does a cow say?"). *All of this engagement is building schemas.* Such parent–child work not only grows our kids' abilities to interact with the outside world, it also shapes and frames for them what the world is like, and how they should see and understand it.

At the earliest ages, then, we need to chatter with them explicitly about skin tone and other kinds of physical differences. Because many of us have been deeply impacted by the practice of silence in white communities, engaging in this kind of chatter may require us to willfully override deep ambivalence about pointing out and talking about racial differences. But this intentional decision, awkward as it may feel as first, is worth it.

If we believe racial differences are beautiful and we want our children to learn to see people of color as beautiful, we have to constantly and early name aloud and describe as beautiful the different colors of skin. Such a practice impacts our children's racial development in several ways. It's a preemptive counter to the negative messaging our children will be exposed to and are at risk of absorbing very early in life.

Such chatter also normalizes a parent-children dialogue about observable physical difference from the earliest stages of our children's awareness of such. It prevents taboos about observing differences from developing and inserting themselves between parents and children. We know that preschool-age children have already begun to assume they should hide their observations about race from adults; they know there's a taboo. So we must signal to them over and over that race talk is welcome.[1] Affirmation that talking about race is welcome cannot be overdone in white culture.

When I say chatter, I mean chatter. If you want some really helpful examples, the highly acclaimed online teaching site *Raising Race Conscious Children* is a great resource.[2] This site is replete with parents describing the ways they chatter about difference with their children. And because the short articles there involve actual dialogues with real kids, you get a sense of how the chatter goes! Dark skin, light skin, brown skin, peach skin. Curly hair, blonde hair, coarse hair, thick hair. These stories also often end up describing amazing conversations that unexpectedly emerge out of such chatter.

To be sure, skin tone differences are not the same thing as race. Suggesting the kind of chatter I've just described doesn't mean we shouldn't also use the language of African American, Black, Latino/a, Native American, and so forth with our children. We should, even when they are too young yet to understand what these categories mean. But it's also true, at even younger ages than race can be understood, that we need to learn to let the language of observing the physical differences roll off of our tongues and become part of the fabric of our everyday conversations. When our children are young they are so deeply engaged in the developmental work of constantly describing the world. Chatter about physical differences should be part of that development.

Obviously this strategy only makes sense with very young kids; this way of naming difference isn't all that relevant to those of us whose children are already older. But even though the method would be different, the principle of preventing or undoing powerful taboos that congeal around race- and difference-talk *does* pertain to older kids. Part of the point of chatter is to prevent silence about race from forming or interrupting it if or as it already has. For those of us with older children who maybe haven't yet used many race-conscious approaches, the same goal exists. We just need to embody it in more age-appropriate ways.

On the one hand the chatter about difference relates directly to a diversity strategy many parents are aware of and may be comfortable with. Namely *it's important we have diverse toys and books in which diversity is represented in our kids' lives.* When we are reading with them, we should point out and have them point out and talk about characters who look different from one another, including observations about features that tend to signify race. If our kids have differently raced dolls, the different features of their dolls should be a topic of our dialogue with them, just as we might talk in a playful way about the kinds of clothes their dolls are wearing.

I can't say enough how important it is that we be explicit. I know this requires some of us to face and persist through really thick and long-standing taboos of our own. We get lots of pressure in white culture even now to not make such differences an object of pointing or explicit dialogue. But having diverse books and dolls alone actually doesn't do much for kids. We have studies that show that being surrounded by diverse images, media, and toys simply doesn't teach children to value diversity.[3] We have to make explicit conversation and pointing out a part of the mix to get any results.

White Isn't *Standard*

It's also important to make sure we're conscious about pointing out and naming light skin (or white people) too. Everybody's skin tone, hair texture, beautiful fingers, and whatever other physical attributes we are noting gets discussed and named. Being intentional about this is important because there's a strong socializing tendency for whiteness to go as an unnamed racial category, so we must counter this formation as well.

We need to talk about "light" skin as one difference among many kinds of difference. Inadvertently treating white as a norm against which other differences are named will create a schema that sees nonwhite as different while seeing light or white as standard. As with so much of race-conscious parenting, therefore, this, too, requires intention. It's not just that our children are taught that white is the norm and everyone else is different. We've been taught to think and speak in such a manner too. Plus, in US contexts, white characters in books, white dolls in children's toy boxes, and white images on television are in the vast majority. It's really easy to miss realizing that we've fallen into the trap of only naming darker skin tones or pointing out difference *when it isn't white*.

Because white gets centered and treated constantly as a default, decentralizing and counteracting that messaging is a critical component of race-conscious parenting. This same principle needs to be given attention and intention when we start teaching our kids to learn the language of race as well (see below).

Race Isn't *Taboo*

On the other hand, outside the world of play the dialogue and chatter I'm describing also affirms and invites our children's inclination to notice difference at whatever point that inclination shows up. This inclination may emerge at different points for different children, depending on a host of factors. But as I've noted, even as we know that children in the United States notice race long before they are aware they are noticing it, we also know that many learn early to hide their race-talk from adults. The social taboos against explicitly discussing difference are strong. Even if we've never knowingly contributed to such taboos, they can easily insert themselves into parent–child interactions without our awareness. Making a commitment to normalize talk about difference preempts the pressures our children experience in a color-blind-obsessed but highly racist culture to treat difference as a taboo.

If our kids notice difference but we've never talked about difference, they will notice that silence. (Indeed, some of our most powerful taboos are ones we internalize without even realizing we were doing so.) And because adults don't always catch it that kids are noticing—since they do so before they have language for it—they may notice silence even when we don't realize we're being silent. In contrast, when our kids consistently experience us bringing observations of difference into the normal, everyday terrain of life they will assume—without realizing they are assuming it—that this is how they should see reality.

There's a helpful comparison here from sexuality educators who are clear how important it is to teach our kids anatomically correct labels for private parts of the body. Teaching children the correct names of all of their body parts has nothing to do with setting them up to do well later in biology class. It's about supporting them in having a healthy and positive view of bodies and sexuality. When we call an elbow an *elbow* but call a vagina a *private part* or a penis a *wee wee* our children notice. They conclude there's something secret and shameful about their genitalia, which easily feeds into larger cultural shame messages about sexuality generally.

> We cannot teach the values and experiences we want our kids to have if we allow taboos to set the dialogue.

In contrast, explicit naming of body parts works against associations of shame. Such practices make it more likely our children can successfully develop a positive view of their bodies and of sexuality. Another benefit is safety. If they don't develop a sense of taboo about their bodies, our kids are more likely to refuse to keep it a secret if they experience a violation of their bodies and boundaries. As educator Kate Ott writes, accurate language about bodies is a way to "support and nurture curiosity while also teaching privacy and respect."[4] We cannot teach the values and experiences we want our kids to have if we allow taboos to set the dialogue.

These insights are helpful when it comes to thinking about taboos about race. We can't teach the values and experiences we want our kids to have if we allow taboos to constrain our dialogue with them. If we don't talk about physical difference, we teach them there is something forbidden, bad, and shameful about difference. On the flip side, there are so many potential benefits of lots of chatter. We name, acknowledge, and are explicit about race because supporting and nurturing our children is part of helping them grow the values and practices we want for them when it comes to race, difference, and racial justice.

From Skin Tone to Race

Chattering about skin or hair is not the same as talking about race. At some point, we also have to also give our children the language of race itself. What does that look like?

Another story, using a different attribute of identity, can help us think about that. When my daughter was in kindergarten she came home one day having learned about Hanukkah. I was impressed because she'd learned about much more than menorahs. She'd gotten a good deal of the story, and in great detail, of a struggle for independence waged by a minoritized, oppressed people and about how oil burning in a lamp well beyond the number of days it should have was a miracle for liberation and freedom.

It became clear as she engaged in her excited, rapid-fire telling of the story, that H. couldn't remember who the people were. After a short stumble as she tried to recall what they were called, she gave up, continued her account, and started referring to the resistors as "Hanukkah people." This incredible history was so vivid and large in her young mind and it just tumbled out. It was beautiful and really sweet. And it also all began to sound like a mythological account. The Hanukkah people to whom she referred over and over in her high-pitched, small-child voice began sounding more like fairies who lived in a far-off land than actual people.

I relished every minute of listening to her tell this story in her very five-year-old, non-Jewish way. And I knew, of course, it was important she learn who and what these people were and are actually called. When H. was totally done with her story, the first thing I did was join her in her excitement. I asked her a lot of questions and kept inviting her to share more. Then at some point I said, "By the way, you know the Hanukkah people? They are actually called Jewish. Jewish people *celebrate* Hanukkah. And guess what? Your friend B. is Jewish. That story about the oil and the miracle is an amazing story about Jewish people, like your friend B.!" She took all of this in and we continued on in our wonderful discussion about Jewish people, Hanukkah, miracles, liberation, and, of course about her friend B., who was very large on her radar those days.

The parallel here is strong. As sweet as this experience was, I wouldn't want my daughter to go around calling Jewish people *Hanukkah people*. Chatter about difference will need active adult engagement to transition into children learning and using appropriate and acceptable language for race.

Until my other daughter was almost six, she often referred to white people as light-skinned people and African Americans as dark-skinned people. As in, one day when I was relaying a conversation I'd had with someone who was Black she asked, "Mama, was he dark-skinned?" This kind of question sounds very different than a parent and child pointing at different characters in a book talking about different skin tone. It was a holdover from our early chatter about difference. But my daughter's language suggested she was starting to use categories and was using dark-skinned as a category grouping.

Her query signaled how important it was for us to move away from the language of dark- and light-skinned and toward explicitly naming race consistently: "Yes, she is Latina." "No, he's white." Or, as in this situation, "Yes, he had dark skin, he's African American. Some people with dark skin are African American." Redirection moves our kids toward talking about race—by learning to use the language and self-naming that people of color have indicated is desirable.

For a number of reasons, the move to support our children as they begin to appropriately use the language of race is more complicated than my experience with my daughter and the Hanukkah people. Identity is complicated. On the one hand, we need to see and acknowledge race and racial identity. At the same time, doing so—especially with young children—always runs the risk of reducing people to labels or implying everyone who shares that identity label *is the same* in some significant way. On top of that, we don't always *know* how people identify.

These risks are real. But they can't be completely avoided. They aren't reduced at all by just not talking about race in order to avoid them. To mitigate the risks as much as we can, we need to intentionally talk about race in nuanced ways. We need to also be mindful, as we do, of emulating and modeling the behavior and language we want our kids to learn.

Imagine my kids and I are in the car, for example. For whatever reason, they are pointing out the window at a pedestrian and are asking or telling me something about her. In the interest of constantly seeking to build race-conscious chatter and dialogue between us, I might say something like this:

"You mean that person with a blue coat on, who has
     light skin—who looks like she might be white?" *or*
"You mean that person carrying a backpack, who
     looks like she might be Latina?"

The *might* here is important. Maybe the person who looks white is actually biracial or Latina. Maybe the person who has brown skin is actually Black or maybe she's Mexican American and identifies as Chicana. We can't account for every possibility in such random, anonymous situations of this sort. But I know I need to use such day-to-day opportunities to continue this ongoing discourse with my children.

More to the point here, in this situation I use the *might* and the multiple descriptors (a backpack and a skin tone) in an attempt to be specific and nuanced in my speech. And if in a less anonymous situation I find out I am mistaken, I take responsibility and model this for my kids too.

In this example, I'm conscious of a tall order here. We want to raise white kids who definitely see race, but who simultaneously don't make assumptions about people because of their race. This is a tall order that goes back to the concern of the mother (in chapter 1) who was worried about her kids starting to put people in racial boxes. There are real contradictions that show up when we are raising kids race-consciously. They can't be completely avoided, but we can seek to mitigate them. "She *might* be Latina!" However imperfectly and with risks that remain nonetheless, this type of specificity aims in both directions—that of seeing race but also not making assumptions about people.

Getting Specific

Have you ever heard a child whose mom was a doctor say that only men can be doctors? There are dangers in race-conscious dialogues, which have to do with children's brains and how susceptible they are, as they make sense of the world, to stereotyping. As essential as early and often race-talk is for nurturing healthy, antiracist white kids, *the ways we do it matter*.

Some studies have found that as early as age three, white children are more likely to describe Black faces as "more angry."[5] Another study has revealed that by first grade, girls are less likely than boys to believe that girls are "really, really smart."[6] Yes, my mother was a physician. And yes, she still repeats the story about how someone asked me, when I was about four years old, if I wanted to be a doctor when I grew up. I looked this adult dead in the eye and said, "I can't. Only boys can be doctors. Girls have to be nurses."

Psychologist Marjorie Rhodes explains that using labels to make generalizations about groups of people can backfire, even if the generalizations are positive. "Generalizations," she writes, "…such as 'Girls can be anything they want,' 'Hispanics live in the Bronx' or 'Muslims eat different foods,' communicate that we can tell what someone is like by knowing her gender, ethnicity or religion."[7]

When young children hear generalizations they conclude "groups mark stable and important differences between individual people."[8] In other words, they start to assume that race can tell you something determinative about a person. So we should be on notice here that the goal of reaching that challenging paradoxical balance of "*see* race" but "don't make *assumptions*" is out of balance in each of Rhodes's examples.

> Speaking and modeling race-conscious postures does not mean making vague generalizations about groups.

If children conclude that generalized grouping is meaningful in this way, their "tendency to view the world through the lens of social stereotypes" is magnified.[9] Given how many negative stereotypes abound about race, gender, and other categories, then, it's no surprise that strengthening the stereotyping tendencies children already have makes it more likely they will internalize negative stereotypes about groups. This is precisely what seems to be going on when girls are the ones by first grade concluding they can't be "really, really smart" or when a child has a mother she knows to be a physician still says that generally, as a group, girls can't be doctors.

Rhodes's findings don't contradict what I'm advocating for in terms of building a race-conscious schema and talking about race early and often. Rather they give insight into how to do it well. Speaking and modeling race-conscious postures does not mean making vague generalizations about groups. In fact, in terms of long-term impact and results, there are better and worse ways to name race early and often when it comes to these risks. Rhodes's work suggests we need to be specific in our language.

So, for example, in response to me as a young daughter denying the ability of women to be doctors, Rhodes would warn against a response of "Of course girls can be doctors! Girls can do anything." Despite this good message, such a response actually further solidifies a child's sense of the strength and meaning of gender categories. This will then continue to be filled more with negative stereotypes about girls than positive ones. Instead, she might suggest a parental response more like:

> "Why do you think that is the case?" *or*
> "Yes, your doctor is a man. But did you notice that
>   doctor who was a woman at the doctor's office last
>   time we were there? Let's look for her next time." *or*
> "What does your mother do for a living?"

These and other open-ended, inquisitive responses can direct a child's attention back to individuals and away from group generalizations. And this can be done even as we still notice and name race (or, in this example, gender).

Something like this was at work in the way I redirected my daughter in response to her Hanukkah people. "The people you're talking about are called Jewish, your friend B. is Jewish, he celebrates Hanukkah." The following types of statements also implement specificity and avoid generalizing language:

"Yes, he happens to be African American."
"I think that young girl might be Latina."
"I went to the doctor today and she was a Black woman."

Or, in response to my daughter when she asked, "Did he have dark skin?" a specific nuanced response: "Yes, he did, he's African American. Although some African American people have really light brown skin and some people have skin much darker than his."

In response to that last statement, my six-year-old might just look at me and say nothing more. Or she might respond by asking me something, disagreeing with me, or making some other type of observation. Whatever she does with my observation in that moment—whether she's interested or ready to verbally engage me or not—*she hears me*. That insight and response thus go into the mix of knitting her race-conscious schema.

Each of these responses notice race in regard to particular people (or experiences) in ways that are race-conscious. But they do so while heeding the caution against responding to our kids with generic teachings like "African American people can do anything."

Finally, I want to be clear that all of this naming of race is not, in and of itself, antiracism! I'm still describing practices that make up some of the proactive and preemptive work we must do to build a race-conscious schema for white kids. That's the "getting started" work here. But this outcome is critical because it's groundwork for developing active antiracism. Children can't learn antiracism if they don't have the practice of observing, naming, and discussing race in their tool kit.

Let's work to break the taboos that we all already live with. Let's interrupt the silence or speak into the ambivalence that is pervasive in white adult culture about naming difference. What I'm describing here are intentional, race-conscious habits we all need to develop in ourselves and build with our children early in their lives.

Doc McStuffins Is Black!

These nuances may feel overwhelming, especially for those of us for whom this is new. On top of this, we continually experience pressure as parents, teachers, and other caregivers to not name race and instead to adopt color-blind approaches to raising children. It's important to name these pressures, because if we do not recognize their presence it's easy to feel like we're alone. Bucking common wisdom is a difficult thing to do. But knowing we're bucking it can help us persist in doing it!

In spring of 2017 a moving story spread about two young

boys—one white, one Black.[10] These good friends decided to get matching haircuts so their teachers couldn't tell them apart. The story was sweet, as was their friendship. The rapid pace with which the story spread suggested something in our culture having to do with a yearning for interracial relationships. But the story also seemed to function as a large-scale endorsement of the false notions that kids don't see color and that this should be the goal. In fact, the white child's mom told media that his "inability to see a difference" was a parental success because "I just taught him to love everyone the same."[11]

It's really easy to over- and wrongly interpret stories like this. It's simply a fact that most children *do* sense awareness of difference by the age of these two boys. Meanwhile, just like a girl child can look at her physician mother and say "girls can't be doctors," it's completely possible that a Black child and white child, both age four, might recognize their skin tones are different and simultaneously still believe a haircut could fool an adult. Four-year-old minds are that creative! And even if these two boys really don't see their differences now, there is no reason to believe that lack of seeing will last.

But my reason for presenting this story here has more to do with reiterating how important it is for those of us attempting to parent race-consciously to recognize the pressures we face. Broad consumption of a story like this speaks volumes about the strength of the cultural belief that it's a win against racism if children don't see color. Such accounts elevate a narrative that good parenting can succeed if we only teach our children similarly. This makes it easy to doubt ourselves when we start swimming against the tide. We need to find ways to create networks of support for ourselves and to connect with other parents to build our collective ability to persist in such swimming.

Another popular example further demonstrates the power of pressures to "not notice"—and it also helps us return to the need to get specific. Doc McStuffins is an African American female character produced by Disney. Emulating her mother, who is a physician, Doc McStuffins heals her stuffed animals when they are sick or injured through the power of her magic stethoscope (and her incredible imagination). She had $500 million in sales in 2013, which makes her an unusual "crossover" hit. In other words, Doc McStuffins isn't just adored by African American girls. Girls and boys from many racial demographics adore her.

In 2014, an article in the *New York Times* explored Doc McStuffins's success. The article emphasized how important her visibility is for young African American children in a media market where positive images of blackness and black femaleness are shamefully few and far between. The article went on to celebrate the evidence that both boys and white kids (girls and boys) embrace her in remarkable numbers. I couldn't agree more with the desire to laud this success.

The same article repeatedly suggested that Doc McStuffins is a crossover hit because white kids *don't see her as Black*. Even her creator, Chris Nee, sees it this way. She was quoted in the piece, "The kids who are of color see her as an African American girl, and that's really big for them. And I think a lot of other kids don't see her color and that's wonderful as well."[12]

This interpretation was so disappointing. First, Nee's comment implies that Black children are somehow more predisposed to naturally notice color when "other kids" (by which Nee means white kids) don't. This is a racially charged description of Black children! And it's unlikely those white kids don't see Doc McStuffins's color. It's much more likely those white kids just don't live in environments where difference and race are part of the flow of conversation with adults; so those adults don't really know what their kids do or do not notice.

Meanwhile, even if those kids don't see her as an African American girl, that wouldn't be "wonderful." Adults celebrating McStuffins in this way should give us pause. If this is the perception among adults, how are we possibly going to enable kids' healthy racial identity development? Stories like these reveal that, as parents, we have some work to do besides building a race-conscious schema with our children. There are some adult-to-adult conversations we need to have urging other parents to reconsider the impulse to celebrate the (false) belief that white kids don't see color. We also need to find support from other people in our own journeys to continually parent against the color-blind tide. That same tide impacts our persistence and also pulls our kids along in it.

Margaret Beale Spencer, a professor of comparative human development, writes of McStuffins's success, "Children's play is serious business. They are getting ideas about who they are from these objects."[13] I know Spencer's right and I suspect you do too. I watch what characters, books, and shows do to the

87

psyche, self-image, and worlds-they-imagine-to-be-possible of my daughters every day.

And that's precisely why it's wonderful if white kids of both genders not only love Doc McStuffins but also see her *specifically* as a Black female and embrace her as such. It's also appropriate developmental support for those of us who have Doc McStuffins in our homes to intentionally activate that recognition with our children. It is important for African American girls to see a powerful and confident character who looks like them. In a society that denigrates blackness and femaleness, the chance for these girls to identify power and confidence with both is, indeed, a kid's toy success.

The stakes are higher for children of color. But it's a success in equal measure for young white daughters—and doubly so if they are sons—to associate power and confidence with blackness and femaleness too!

So let's be specific. When we talk about Doc McStuffins, let's talk about her brilliance, her kindness, her being a girl, her imagination, her being Black, her healing gifts with toys and stuffed animals, the fact her mom is a doctor, and on and on. Notice how different this is than saying to a two-year-old, "Black people can be doctors too"? Specifying and appreciating Doc McStuffins, blackness, brilliance, girlness, and wonderfulness all in our dialogue with our children is where we begin.

When my kids think they see black and female manifested as powerful and confident, my job is to say this: "Why yes, yes, you do. That is precisely what you are seeing here—an awesome, smart kid like you who has beautiful brown skin." Or when my kids see Black and female manifested as brilliant and creative, but haven't thought to name the Black and female parts aloud yet, my words naming these aloud might invite them to notice that they'd noticed this too. And suddenly we're in a conversation knitting a race-conscious schema together one more time.

Fortitude As It Gets Harder

It may seem a long distance from Doc McStuffins to a protest about police brutality. But the focus on schema I'm introducing here raises an early challenge for parents. If we're speaking authentically about race in the United States we are almost always—or are quickly thereafter—also speaking about oppression and injustice. How much, how early, and in what detail do we expose our children to the realities of injustice? How do we respond when educating our children about what's actually going on in our neighborhoods, cities, and nation means discussing human suffering and violence? These are difficult questions with no one right or wrong answer.

Knitting together a race-conscious schema for the purpose of healthy white identity development (see chapter 3), however, must include attention to and teaching about racial injustice and inequity as much as it does racial difference. If it doesn't, our dialogues will only support "valuing diversity." The unique complexities white children experience and notice about being privileged, insulated, or taught that they are superior will go unaddressed by us and internalized by our kids.

Yet—as with building a schema in which difference is simply assumed to be worth embracing long before our children can conceptually understand that's what they are learning—they also learn about injustice long before they'll have cognitive capacity or categories to discuss it abstractly. In this way, then, my decision to take my young kids to protest the killing of Michael Brown in Ferguson was, among other things, an example of a proactive choice to offer healthy racial identity support.

I had deliberated over whether or not to take them. We have to make careful judgments about whether or how to engage our children in dialogues about realities so serious, heavy, and frightening that they may be simply too much for them. Even after I decided to do so, I chose not to tell them Michael Brown had been killed. I did go emotionally prepared for the possibility that they might overhear explicit statements at the protest itself and that I might end up needing to talk with them more fully about what actually happened, however.

But despite being aware of the risk my children would hear more about intense and violent truths than I might have chosen to introduce otherwise, I concluded that taking them was important. This was primarily a value-based decision for me about showing up as a family with other members of my community to protest police violence. But for my children it had additional function. It was an experiential introduction to the reality of racial injustice in a manner that words (especially at their age) simply didn't allow. It introduced them to the severity of racism in a context in which I was simultaneously modeling my commitments to acting and engaging with others for racial justice. That my children were still too young to discuss any such realities and commitments primarily with words actually made it seem even more important for shaping their racial schema.

Meanwhile, I also knew the protest was the kind of experience that might create an opportunity for a discussion about racial justice. If that happened, my goal would be to follow their lead in terms of what they did or didn't understand, and might need or want explained after our shared experience. And in a challenging way, it did do that, as you saw in my opening story.

Experiences like the protest are an example of proactively shaping our children's schema for understanding injustice and resistance in ways that precede their ability to understand racism conceptually. A protest teaches and forms schema by providing an actual experience of an environment where difference abounds, but within which discussions of injustice and embodied resistance simply *are* the landscape. People gathering in solidarity became a part of my daughters' basic, experiential sense of reality that day.

Of course, such experiential learning must be repeated and sustained to have an impact. Still, this type of learning shapes a schema that is race- and justice-conscious rather than one that presumes sameness and equity. Subsequently, as children become able to intellectually explore issues of racism, these explorations unfold against a backdrop in which they are already deeply equipped and familiar with the reality of pervasive social, racial inequity.

When we went to the protest, I didn't insist my children listen carefully or stay quiet. But I also stayed near the edge of the crowd so they could move around and wouldn't bother others.

My older daughter found her way to some concrete steps and enjoyed swinging around on the banister.

And then, of course, the experience unfolded and raised some of the same insights and challenges of children noticing race in the grocery story. Given our fraught racial environments, white children speaking aloud in public about and pointing out race almost always creates discomfort. "Black people aren't safe! But we're white, so *we're* safe! Right [Mama]?" Ugh.

As we commit to cultivating a race- and justice-conscious schema, parents of white children breaking silence around race have to come to terms with at least two things. First, there is so much we do not control about what children say, and when or how loudly they say it. Second, as our children come to voice in ways we can't control, they will do more than just notice difference. If and as we are teaching them about actual US racial realities and supporting them in naming, analyzing, and interpreting their own actual experiences, they *are* going to voice their recognition of being white and having privilege. That's what happened with my daughter at the protest.

This second point connects directly with the specific challenge that the long-term habit of white silence on race has created. The complexity of being white in a white racial hierarchy juxtaposed with the reality that children will say anything, anywhere, truly ups the ante of how daunting race-talk with white kids can be. Young white children learning that racial injustice is a reality and, simultaneously, learning the language of race are going to make the connection that their white identity insulates them from injustice.

The example above is a case in point: my daughter essentially announced a very loud and public "*oh . . . whew!*" in regard to her/our white privilege and white protection. Worse, she did so in a public space where Black and Latino/a people were protesting and mourning precisely the lack of such protection for their families.

My daughter's public vocalization of awareness of her own safety as it related to her whiteness was easily the most anxiety-inducing part of this experience. Yet while this moment was uncomfortable, understanding the long-view significance of my daughter's vocalization as being in the interest of her own development of a healthy white racial identity enabled me to persist in a race-conscious stance.

One of the biggest impediments to healthy white identity is "white guilt," which results from the experience of moral dissonance: from being white and benefiting from injustice while believing equality *should be* the state of things. White Americans tend to treat this dimension of our experience as something like a dirty secret. This dirty secret contributes mightily to our being silent when we should speak, as well as impeding our ability to learn to engage well with race. (In fact, white guilt is so powerful that its impact on healthy white racial identity development is one of the most important things we're going to talk about in the next chapter.)

Children's aloud assessments of their own experiences of this racialized society proactively and powerfully equip them, initiating significant longitudinal learning. It takes a long time to develop the capacity to speak about race and its function in the social environment. It takes longer to emotionally navigate the moral quagmire that being white creates. It cannot be overstated, then, what a positive move it is to have young white children begin to name this complexity ("we're white so we're safe!"), *rather than internalizing the dirty secret.*

This doesn't mean we leave them there! In the moment with my daughter, my goals included not shaming or embarrassing her while also respecting those who might have overheard her. In this case, that meant leaning down and quietly saying to her, "Yes, we are white, but let's talk about this in the car. Right now we need to listen. Okay?" My tone was even-keeled and warm. It conveyed no anxiety or sense she'd done something wrong.

In the car, I invited her back into conversation. "Remember how you noticed people saying Black people aren't safe? But we're white so we are?" "Uh-huh," she said. "Well," I said, "you're right, we're white and that does keep us more safe. And the whole reason we went to that protest was because we really want everyone to be safe. I want Black people to be just as safe as white people."

"Yes," she said. "I want it too!"

The goal is to minimize the amount of time they experience internalizing and interpreting without adult support. One way we accomplish this is by introducing the *reality* of the existence of racial inequity early. We want to be present for and explicitly journey with them, interpreting, engaging, and exploring further questions and insights. Starting early offers our children proactive support to move toward healthy racial identity, the specific contours of which will be the focus of the next chapter.

Takeaways

✓ It is difficult for many white adults to begin
to speak about race openly and explicitly. We
only learn to do it and get better at it through
practice. There's no way around those awkward, challenging feelings.

✓ There's no special age at which point kids
are ready to hear and understand the difficult
truths about race and racism. They begin to
work out their racial concepts and ideas long
before they can articulate them.

✓ We start with our children's deepest assumptions about the world: a notion of race as visible and normal, an awareness of racial injustice, and a working presumption that people
can and do take actions against racism.

✓ Young children should be engaged with lots
of talk about difference: skin tone and bodies,
and the ways different communities of color
identify. Making a commitment to normalize
talk about difference preempts the pressures
kids experience to treat *difference* as a taboo.

✓ Be aware that using the language of race—especially with young children—always runs the risk of reducing people to labels or implying everyone who shares that identity label *is the same* in some significant way (stereotyping). Be specific and nuanced.

✓ Race-conscious parenting for a healthy white identity development must include teaching about racial *injustice and inequity* as much as it does racial *difference*. Consider experiential learning, such as protests, for this.

CHAPTER 3

What Does a "Healthy" White Kid Look Like?

"I was so relieved when my second grader came home excited about everything she had learned during her school's Martin Luther King Jr. Day celebration. I'd worried about what she would be taught, and was ready to fill in the blanks. Like, I figured they might sugarcoat things. But when my daughter came home, she was not only excited about what she had learned but her school had done a great job. But then, after she'd eagerly shared with me all that she'd learned, my daughter said to me, 'You know what, Mom? I'm so glad we're white!' And I thought, Oh my god! Do we say that?"

Many challenges show up when we start talking about race in explicit ways with white children. Imagine if this mother's child had been Latina or Native American and had come home after celebrating a day devoted to a powerful leader within the Latino/a community or a justice movement led by Native peoples and said, "I'm so glad we're Latinas!" or "I'm so glad to be Native American." I think it's likely her mother's response would not have been "Oh my god!" Perhaps Black children in that same second-grade class did go home that day and eagerly responded to their learning with "You know what, Mom? I'm so glad we're Black!" I can imagine the parental response to these children might have been, "Indeed!" But white declaration of gratitude for being white throws into sharp relief a very different landscape. This landscape is full of awkwardness that is unique to parenting white children.

This "I'm so glad I'm white!" story allows us to engage the question of what we are aiming for in the long term by raising white children in a race-conscious manner. I want to put the question in this way: "What does a *healthy* white kid look like, anyway?"

In some ways, the answer to that question is straightforward. Healthy white children are children who have been nurtured over time to be comfortable in their own skin but who are also able to function well and appropriately in racially diverse environments. They are children who neither ignore nor pretend not to notice the racial identities of others but who also do not make assumptions about people based on their race. They are children who feel equipped and have strong moral commitments to interrupt and challenge racism when they witness it, both in interpersonal and day-to-day life moments, as well as in its larger structural and societal forms.

This is all a tall order in a nation that doesn't talk about race very well. It's also an order that seems full of contradictions. Can you simultaneously honor race as meaningful but not make assumptions about what it means when you see it?

What does that even look like? Can a child be learning anti-racism if he/she isn't old enough to quite explain what racism is? It turns out that the answer to "What does a 'healthy' white kid look like?" is not straightforward after all.

Complexities attend the notion of "healthy identity" in regard to white people generally, regardless of age. The specificity of these complexities is the very reason this book is called *Raising White Kids* and not just *Raising Kids*. When it comes to teaching them to value equity and justice, white children are in a position distinct from their peers of color. That positioning brings unique difficulties. They are being raised and educated in a society in which they, because of their racial identity, are located on top. They are treated better. They are given messages about their superiority. They are treated as if they are the norm and rewarded for being white on a regular basis in ways that are both overt and subtle. It's white positioning, then, that makes the question of what healthy racial identity is for white people complex.

White racial identity development theory can help us explore this complexity. It offers a developmental model to consider what healthy racial identity is and how parents can best nurture its growth.

It would be understandable if the mother in this story responded to her second-grader, "No, actually, *we don't say* 'I'm so glad we're white!'" Such a response might reduce her anxiety about the likely possibility her daughter will go out and make such a statement again in a context in which it would raise some eyebrows. And, of course, a healthy white kid is not a child who is still running around at the age of twenty gleefully announcing, "I'm so glad I'm white."

But responding to this young child's announcement with a declarative no would not offer her the racial nurture she needs. Moreover, from a developmental perspective this second-grade declaration might actually be understood as evidence of racial health on display. Instead, a race-conscious parenting approach, rooted in understanding of white racial identity development, can enable this mother to engage her child in ways that recognize what is developmentally positive about her daughter's declaration. Then she will be more prepared to support her to further that development.

Our ability to understand the paradoxes that are normal, predictable dimensions of raising race-conscious white kids in a racist society and to make intentional choices in response is deepened by knowledge of racial development. Such knowledge helps us recognize common landmarks in the white experience in anticipation of which we can be proactive and in regard to which we can be responsive. White children are living in a society that is racially hierarchical, divided, and unjust. It seeks to draw white people into collusion with hierarchy and injustice every step along the way. The goal is to maximize our positive impact on the growth of such children and youth given this difficult context. All of this, then, is what this chapter is about.

White Racial Identity Development

As a theory of human development, racial identity development theory comes from the world of psychology. Racial identity development theories presume that just as human beings develop physically, emotionally, and intellectually, we also develop racially. Psychologists who work in this area of study have identified and described various stages of racial development for different racial groups.

If we understand racial development to be part of human development, it makes perfect sense that knowing something about it would be important for parents and others who want to be an influence in raising healthy white children. Physical development is, at least in part, an internal and embodied response to the effect of things like nutrition, exercise, and vitamins. Intellectual development is impacted by engagement with visual, linguistic, and written information. In the same way, racial identity develops as one moves through and in response to various racial environments, experiences, and messages. So whether it's knowing the nutritional content of Cheerios, the benefits of learning phonics, or the way moral vision is activated when we celebrate antiracist heroes and sheroes, those of us who shape those environments, experiences, and messages need to know something about development.

I want to underline the point that we're talking about a relationship between the internal and external. We're not talking about racial identity being indicative of innate differences among different racial groups. Race does not predetermine or predispose who we become or how we grow. Rather there is constant interaction between the internal selfhood and the external world; interaction produces certain tendencies in racial development. External environments and experiences, and the interpretations and explanations we offer in response to these, show up in human self-understanding, the shape of our emotional lives, our future responses to racism, and so forth.

Moreover, we are talking only about tendencies. Like any kind of development, the way white people respond to environments and experiences varies. It's not completely predictable. We are all individuals with different stories and personalities. How I respond to an encounter may be different than the way you do. Still, interactions can create overarching similarities and patterns, in regard to which awareness of racial identity development can be of great help as we engage children.

I also want to underline the point that whether we explicitly pay attention to children's racial development or not, our children develop anyway. So for those of us who want to raise white children who are able, facile, and engaged as friends, peers, and citizens in a diverse society, paying intentional attention to racial development isn't optional. We can't just put our best foot forward, push off hard conversations about race for fear that we won't do a good enough job or generically teach them the value of equality, and then hope for the best. If we don't pay attention and nurture children explicitly, the external environments in which our children are exposed daily to racialized messages will do the shaping in our absence.

In fact, simply recognizing the existence of racial identity development as a phenomenon is helpful in and of itself. Again, consider a parallel. Because we know that children develop physically, most of us would never expect a desirable outcome if we allowed our young children to make their own choices about food. We know if we did this, most kids—if they're anything like mine—would eat a ton of sugar! The impact on their physical development would be profound. We also know that just messaging them that they *should* like vegetables would not cause them, on their own, to choose to eat vegetables. So—armed with a basic understanding that the body changes in response to what it consumes—many parents insist on peas.

In a similar way, awareness that racial identity develops over time and is an unavoidable human process in a racialized society inclines us to pay attention to it. Understanding that racial identity unfolds and grows in our kids' lives, even if we don't quite grasp all of the ins and outs of what this looks like or always know how best to nurture it, inclines us to begin to notice things we otherwise might not.

But we can go further, of course, and learn explicitly about the developmental tendencies of white US Americans. For these purposes, Janet Helms and Beverly Daniel Tatum, both psychologists who happen to be African American, are among the most accessible of the experts who have engaged in extensive study of racial identity development.

Both Helms and Tatum have written several great books. But two of my favorites are Helms's book *A Race Is a Nice Thing to Have: A Guide to Being a White Person or Understanding the White Persons in Your Life* and Tatum's book *"Why Are All the Black Kids Sitting Together in the Cafeteria?" And Other Conversations About Race.*[1] (The titles alone show what great reads these books are!)

I draw on both of these psychologists to provide an overview of white development, which will inform our conversation about healthy white identity. But the specific labels I'm using belong to Helms. For the purpose of being able to talk about general patterns in white development, Helms has identified six stages of white identity. These stages are:

- Contact
- Disintegration
- Reintegration
- Pseudo-Independence
- Immersion/Emersion
- Autonomy[2]

In Helm's taxonomy (and Tatum agrees, using slightly different language), we all begin in Contact stage. The hope is that over the course of our lives we will develop toward and into Autonomy stage.

Before we get any further, I want to say that talking about stages of racial identity development can be deceptive. On the one hand, the dispositions and behaviors that tend to show up in white people as we grow toward autonomy are precisely the kinds of characteristics race-conscious parenting aspires to cultivate in children. Also, having a sense of what white growth often looks like along the way is useful. It helps us have a better conversation about antiracist development; what it looks like and how we get there.

But we need to be careful. To use the language of stages is to use a tool. And a tool is just that: only a tool. Stages are not supposed to be used as some kind of diagnosis of all white behavior (or people!). They shouldn't be stamped on ourselves, or others, the way we might use a cookie cutter to impose a predetermined shape.

Also, as we'll see in the scenarios discussed below, development can look very different from one person to the next. This can be true even among people roughly moving through the same stage of identity development. For one thing, racial growth can occur at such different ages. Racial identity is not a set of life stages that can be closely associated with chronological age. Endless variations in human life impact how and when people grow, move through, or even remain stuck in, various stages. Where one lives, who's in one's family, what messages one gets from trusted adults and how often, what is regularly on the television, who is in one's classroom—all of these variables impact when and how our environmental experiences with race and racism transpire.

For another thing, racial development is not a linear process. Nor are the various stages mutually exclusive. We can actually experience more than one at the same time. It's probably better to understand these stages as landmarks. They are points in life, learning, and experiences at which tendencies often appear. But, again, these tendencies look different in different people. The stages are not firm, fixed, or static. And any one of us can experience growth into one stage of identity, only to go back to a prior developmental stage if certain conditions present themselves.

For example, as an adult I spent almost ten years engaged

in activism and committed antiracism work in New York City. I learned there to function alongside and in support of African American and Latino/a activists challenging police brutality. I taught "whiteness" and racial justice to multiracial groups of graduate students. I became very comfortable talking about race and racial justice in racially diverse settings—even when such talk became uncomfortable. I was experiencing immersion/emersion.

But when I moved to the demographically predominantly white state of Iowa in 2004, within only a couple of years I noticed how differently I'd begun to experience my own white identity. I was less comfortable in my own skin in a room of mostly people of color than I had been when such spaces had been a very regular part of my daily life. I found myself worrying that I might say or do the wrong thing and was more tentative about taking the risk to do so. It was like I had gotten out of practice. I seemed to have moved back to somewhere in between reintegration and pseudo-independence.

That experience is indicative of just how nonlinear and fluid racial development is. Development is a constant process and unless we are continually active on the journey, we can easily move backward into earlier stages of development and understanding.

Mapping out stages of white identity development is useful as long as we don't ask it to do something it was never intended to do. It gives us a way to see behaviors many white people manifest and better understand emotional challenges many of us go through as we journey toward antiracist commitment. By helping us better understand these, it helps us strategize how to enable development toward autonomy. Most important, it gives us a way to talk together about what it is we're aiming for when we're parenting race consciously. Namely, it gives us some answers to the question, what does a *healthy* white kid look like anyway?

From Contact to Disintegration: What Do You Mean We're Not All Equal?

Tatum and Helms suggest that at the earliest developmental stage, white people tend to believe things are racially fine in society and that our collective declaration of "Everybody is equal" actually describes the way things are. Prior to having had direct experiences or noticed evidence to the contrary, race is not perceived to be a particular meaningful category. It certainly isn't perceived as meaning anything significant relative to questions about justice or fairness. At this stage, as well, racial difference is even simply accepted as a positive and normal aspect of human experience, even if one hasn't given much thought to any of this.

It's inevitable, however, that at some point white people encounter experiences in which people are treated differently because of race. So such dispositions and beliefs begin to ebb. When we have such encounters at a frequency or intensity with which they can no longer be ignored, the prior "naive belief" that race is not meaningful starts to disintegrate. We move from what Helms calls Contact stage into Disintegration stage. Disintegration may begin in a young child when he's out on a playground and overhears racial teasing. He struggles to understand why white children would behave in such a way or appreciate why a child of color gets upset. My first-grade experience outside the bathroom might be understood as an example of movement into disintegration. In that case, it was not so much that I saw racially unjust treatment. But I was definitely jarred into a stark recognition that there was something meaningful, loaded, and emotionally dangerous about racial difference. I was jarred first as a new self-recognition dawned on me when J. invited me to start a white girls club. I was jarred again when my white teacher made clear J. and I had done something bad.

Disintegration can also take place when we're older. I've seen it occur in white college students when they are presented with videos of Black youth describing their encounters with police officers and the regularity, intensity, and impact of such encounters in their day-to-day lives. Having thought things were mostly fine, or at least so much better because of the civil rights movement, grappling with powerful and irrefutable first-person testimonies to the contrary can cause these prior assumptions and frameworks to unravel.

But full-grown adults can experience disintegration too. After the election of Donald Trump, for example, one of my friends sent me a string of texts over several weeks. He was so shocked that people would actually vote for someone who said such racially vitriolic things that he abruptly arrived at a radically new recognition of how pervasive racism is in the United States. He began to see racial disparities everywhere—at the local car wash in the disparity between who was washing the cars and who was driving them; at his workplace in who had the high-paying jobs and who cleaned the bathrooms. This new vision brought him emotional distress, which led to his repeated texts. He realized he'd never seen clearly what now seemed impossible to not see, and was face-to-face with a painful recognition that our nation simply wasn't what he'd thought it was before November 2016.

However different it may look from one person to another, the stakes in white identity development are high at this point. We disintegrate because we have an encounter in which the moral dilemmas posed by racism become impossible to ignore or deny. In effect, this means our existing framework for interpreting reality—a framework predicated on a simplistic belief in equality and sameness—is shattered. It doesn't work anymore. And because humans don't function without interpretive frameworks, once that happens we have to respond.

Moreover, as can be seen in my students or my friend, disintegration often brings stress. Helms says it's a state of "high dissonance." Part of the reason is that so many unplanned racial encounters in the United States are negative ones. Another reason is that any unanticipated shattering of a prior interpretative framework (racial or otherwise) causes stress. When we experience a fundamental disruption of what we have assumed to be true and have used to explain reality, we are left with the challenge of completely reorienting our minds, hearts, and emotions. That's stressful.

Between the need for an interpretative framework and the desire to resolve the stress of dissonance, motivation to move through disintegration can be very strong. One might do a full retreat to Contact stage—something like putting one's hands over one's ears and eyes and repeating loudly, "I didn't see it! I can't hear it!"

I am fairly sure, for example, that's precisely what I did after my encounter with Ms. B. I shrank back to Contact stage about as quickly as someone who touches a hot stove snatches back her hand. I was still young enough at the time and had not yet had many such experiences. I was thus able, at least partially, to return to a place of willful naiveté, as if the exchange had never happened. This is a perfect example that reminds us identity development isn't linear.

But the options forward and through disintegration are either to reintegrate the experience of racially differential treatment into our prior framework or to embark on the more difficult and uncertain work of creating a new framework. This is a critical moment, because the outcomes of this choice lead to radically different postures toward racism and racial justice. The way we respond to evidence of racism could not be more different depending on whether we move toward reintegration or pseudo-independence.

Reintegration Stage: Blaming People of Color

If I attempt to reintegrate the experience of differential treatment into my prior framework—the one that presumes things are basically fine in society—I have no choice but to explain the experience of people being treated differently because of race by justifying it in some way. And so, to put it bluntly, I blame people of color for differential treatment. This goes like this in the reintegrating white mind: If Black people are shot by police at higher rates than whites, they must be more dangerous or prone to criminal behavior and deserving of such treatment. If Latino/a people are suffering economically and doing the lowest-paying work, they must be lazy and, thus, their poverty is a natural result of such laziness.

Reintegration stage is movement along a pathway that embraces or internalizes various justifications for racial disparities and inequity. Such embrace may not always be conscious—racialized, racist justifications for why people of color experience racism may run deep and can be implicit or subtle. But reintegrating means accepting at some level the false belief that white people are superior and do well or are treated well because we deserve it, and that people of color are inferior and don't.

Reintegration is often accompanied by fear of or anger toward people of color. We might try to avoid being around African Americans or Latinos, or may actively participate in exclusion and discrimination. We can make such moves without ever resorting explicitly to the language of race and may exhibit behaviors that fall along a continuum. One person may maintain individual relationships with specific Black or Latino/a people whom they treat or see as "exceptional," as in "not really Black." In fact, this way of treating African Americans may have been one reason it was possible for President Barack Obama to be elected in a nation in which

> Difficult questions about one's identity begin to surface as we recognize white participation in racism.

racial bias remains rampant. In many ways, he was framed as an "exceptional" Black person.[3] But reintegration also shows up in the most obviously objectionable and explicitly racist forms, from whites who actively deny people of color access to resources (such as jobs), to those who commit acts of verbal harassment or physical violence.

Pseudo-Independent Stage: Something Is Wrong with Society

Instead of reintegration, a very different path is pursued if one moves out of disintegration and seeks out or creates a new interpretative framework after the disruption of encountering racism. In Pseudo-Independent stage white people conclude this: if racially disparate treatment exists, then the prior framework was wrong. Something must be wrong with society after all. Our systems must be unjust and inequitable. In response I become motivated to better understand what's actually going on and to learn about structural racism and how it functions.

Pseudo-independence brings many new possibilities because it involves the creation of a new framework for understanding reality. This framework takes seriously the idea that society is structured by racism. Recognizing racial injustice as structural and perpetuated by white people is an opportunity for intellectual growth. Powerful positive emotions can attend this growth because we begin to find some language and analysis for phenomena we've experienced. We begin to better understand experiences we knew indicated that something was not quite right, but in regard to which we didn't have language.

I remember, for example, reading James Cone's book *Black Theology of Liberation* for the first time when I was about nineteen years old. Cone's work can be hard for white people. It's a no-holds-barred critique of the complacency toward and participation of white people in white supremacy. But when I read it, I experienced the profound relief of waking up. I'd been troubled throughout high school that in my robustly multiracial school my advanced placement classes were almost exclusively white. I knew something was wrong. I'd noticed that the classrooms I'd been in from first through sixth grade, which had started out as mostly students of color, had gotten whiter and whiter since middle school. But I had no way to explain or even ask about this troubling observation. Cone's work unexpectedly gave me language and explained for me what I was experiencing. Such an unflinching exposure of the effects of social white supremacy was truly awful. But the ability to now see and understand what I had only before felt was a huge relief.

That said, pseudo-independence can also bring stress. To recognize society is responsible for racial injustice, that systemic injustice benefits whites, and that people like us—including people we love and admire—perpetuate it is truly distressing. It can induce in us anger at other white people. We might try to create distance from them and decide we are better than most other whites. It might invoke shame. Not yet having a developed sense of who we are or how we understand ourselves now in the midst of such recognition, we start to worry about what structural injustice means for our own moral complicity. Are white people only bad? Always bad? Does that mean I am bad?

Pseudo-independence invites deeper reflection and journey and is a desirable outgrowth of disintegration. But it's still an early developmental stage. Difficult questions about one's identity begin to surface as we recognize white participation in racism. But few of us have yet developed the skills or found paths on which to walk through such questions. Nor do most of us have ready access to white models who might show us how to explore and respond to these questions.

The disjuncture here has to do with the gap between emotional and intellectual understanding. Intellectual understanding often comes more quickly than emotional understanding. It takes longer to process and work through the complicated emotional experiences that cognitive understanding of the impact of structural racism as a white-perpetuated and pervasive social reality generates. The common phenomenon of "white guilt" is a perfect example of what can manifest as a result of such emotional/intellectual disjuncture. If you believe in equity but intellectually recognize that inequity is the norm and that you directly benefit from inequity, injustice, and even violence, it's understandable you might begin to feel guilty! In fact, to return to our opening story, depending precisely on how the lessons were taught and what stories were told, that white second-grader could have just as

> People of color often experience white guilt as a selfish and self-indulgent emotional state. It doesn't help them end racism, and it's draining to be around.

easily come home on that school day and instead of announcing "I'm so glad we're white!" she might have asked "Why are white people so bad?" Or "Are all white people bad?"

A developmental perspective helps us recognize that white guilt is a normal and predictable part of a white development. But it also helps us see how important it is for white people to work through. White guilt is normal, but it doesn't help us engage in active, agency-filled antiracist action. It's normal but it doesn't help in the fight to end racism. In fact, people of color often experience white guilt as a selfish and self-indulgent emotional state. It doesn't help them end racism and it's draining to be around. The emotional responses of whites during pseudo-independence, then, can make sustained and authentic interracial relationships really difficult.

Another challenging emotion in pseudo-independence is fear. Even as my understanding of racism is growing at a rapid rate, I may not have a lot of experience in or knowledge of how to talk about race. I haven't yet built emotional resilience for engaging with others about it. When I ask my college students why race is so hard to talk about, for example, white students always say they're terrified they'll say something racist. Ironically, increased awareness of and concern about racism can actually immobilize white people because we become more aware of the risk of saying or doing something racist and more conscious of the harm this causes people of color.

Guilt and fear are unpleasant. Living with them without a sense of how to move through them productively can be exhausting. These and other stresses rooted in the moral dilemmas of becoming newly racially aware can cause us to revert or regress back to prior stages. Instead of staying and wrestling with the uncomfortable feelings that come with recognizing white privilege we externalize these difficult recognitions. Adopting interpretations that explain racism away or downplaying how much one person can do to challenge it are temptations. These responses seem easier than facing and moving through challenging emotions. If guilt is left unresolved, it can turn into anger and be directed outward toward people of color. We may start to get frustrated when people of color in our workplaces or other contexts bring up racism again. We get tired of it, partly because we see that we are complicit, aren't sure what to do about it, and so—sometimes—just rather it would all go away.

But all of these possibilities are precisely why developmental awareness and work is so important. We need strategies and support to push through to what Helms has called Immersion/Emersion stage. So will our children.

On the flip side, the stresses of pseudo-independence can instead be powerful motivation to continue to search and journey forward toward racial health. Some of us respond, therefore, by immersing ourselves in these challenges and do so to great benefit.

Immersion/Emersion Stage: Changing My Relationship to Whiteness

When white people start to realize we can explore, challenge, and change the meaning of race in our own lives, we manifest movement into Immersion stage. We realize we can

116

ask questions like "Who am I racially?" and "Who do I want to be?" We move from experiencing being white in a reductive sense—as in, I-am-innately-only-bad-and-always-racist. Instead, we still recognize racism continues to have profound power in our lives, but we also see that we can complicate our relationship to our own whiteness. We begin to realize that actively committing to antiracism changes the experience and feel of that relationship. We learn there are ways to discover and create different answers to such questions than those we've perhaps been given from white people around us.

In immersion, these questions don't signal being deluded into the false idea I can escape my whiteness. I can never ignore my positioning as a white person in society. (This is not the same thing as saying, "Race doesn't matter; I can be whatever I want it to be.") Exploring identity is a process of deepening my understanding of the significance and impact of whiteness in my life and in the world around me. I come to realize that I have the ability to *impact and challenge* the power of racism in my life and can participate in antiracist resistance to it. I may begin to submerge myself in work against racism, take increasing risks against it, speak up more often to challenge it, join with others in organized justice struggles.

Immersion may also mean emotional understanding starts to catch up with intellectual understanding. We might start to make sense out of difficult feelings we've experienced in prior racial experiences or that emerge in new ones. For example, it was work on identity that helped me better understand my experience outside the bathroom door in first grade; I recognized the shame my teacher's response had elicited in me and how this had made me much more afraid to engage race intentionally for so long. Processing feelings from prior or ongoing experience can reduce the residual impact of such emotions in our lives.

Doing such work helps us become more emotionally resilient in present experiences. If I've worked through shame and guilt I am much more emotionally able to take in critical feedback and take it seriously. I am more eager and able to work to improve my behavior when I am challenged and told I've done something racist or behaved in a manner in which white privilege is clearly operative. In contrast, in earlier developmental stages such critical feedback—according to Tatum—feels more like "getting punched in the stomach or called a 'low-life scum.'"[4] What I hear is, "Yep, because I'm white I can only be bad," especially if a person of color challenges me. And when this is how I feel, I'm much more likely to get defensive, cry, or run away if I am critiqued. But in immersion I begin to be able to see the possibility for my own growth and change, and to recognize that while I am deeply implicated in racism as a white person, I do not have to be reduced to *only* being racist just because I am white.

A particularly important recognition in immersion/emersion is that we have our own stake in antiracism work as white people. Prior to this developmental point, white people are more likely to think we should fight racism for the sake of people of color. That view is more likely to lead us into actions that are patronizing, condescending, or otherwise fail to recognize the full humanity of people of color.

Of course, the violence and harm people of color experience because of racism is primary and the most urgent moral reason to fight it. But white people do have our own stake. Anne Braden, a journalist and a powerful Southern white anti-racist activist during the civil rights movement and beyond, put it this way: "White people need to begin to challenge racism as if our lives depended on it, because they do."[5] White supremacy malforms my humanity, constrains my life, compromises my spirit. When I recognize this I begin to see the fight against racism as also a life-giving struggle for my own liberation. This shift may also signal a move from guilt to anger—a kind of healthy moral anger at injustice and an outrage that people of color are being harmed, combined with the recognition that it's being done in my name.

Autonomy Stage: An Ongoing Journey

The final developmental stage is Autonomy. Despite Helms's choice of labeling, this doesn't mean we have no need for others. We can't successfully function individualistically and in isolation in regard to race and racism. It's more like having our feet firmly planted on the ground in a more holistic way. We don't need to either denigrate people of color based on race nor to falsely idealize or romanticize them. We remain continually open to and desirous of learning. We seek to constantly learn from people who are different from ourselves because we know we will grow if we do.

Here, we understand white racial growth and antiracist commitment must always remain a journey. It is never over. And we become increasingly aware of the complexities of racism, the ways that racism and sexism interact with each other.

We become more able to apologize and take responsibility when we make mistakes in regard to race, without feeling as though our very core self is being somehow deemed unworthy.

Autonomy is a developmental state in which we have grown enough to have some accurate sense of our own abilities, agency, facility, and language around race and antiracism. We are less likely to feel we always need to wait to challenge racism only after we see people of color do it first, or first ask them how we should do it. Instead we recognize it's our moral obligation to challenge racism and to continually develop our skills at doing so. At the same time, however, we also recognize the need to constantly stay accountable to people of color. We realize white people need to grow our antiracist resistance in response to what people of color continue to say and teach about racism and resistance to

> White racial growth and antiracist commitment must always remain a journey.

it. Being constantly aware of the powerful and ongoing ways being white shapes me in a racist society leads me to remain committed to constantly checking in, learning more, and being open to critical feedback from and to the leadership of people of color.

So What Is a Healthy White Racial Identity?

The section above is a big-picture overview of white racial identity development, a general description of how it often proceeds and a sense of some of its significant landmarks. Let's return now to the question of healthy white racial identity so we can begin to explore how an understanding of "healthy" can undergird the choices and moves we make to nurture white children in their racial understanding.

The most important word to hold on to here is *paradox*. Healthy white identity does not mean teaching children to embrace their whiteness and celebrate "White is beautiful!" It does not mean lifting up whiteness as one difference amid a multicultural array of differences. In a society structured as a white racial hierarchy in which violence and injustice against people of color are the norm, such teaching is morally incoherent.

> None of us, regardless of our racial identity, can be truly racially healthy as long as we live in a racist society.

Similarly, healthy does not mean pretending any of us is "just human." We can't simply disavow our whiteness nor pretend being white does not impact our humanness as part of our effort to disavow racism or challenge racial hierarchy. So on the one hand, aiming for racial health means we need to teach white children they are white. Our children need to be taught that their whiteness does position them in specific ways relative to racism and their relationships with children of color.

But on the other hand, healthy does not mean wandering around wracked with guilt and feeling uncomfortable in one's skin all the time. It doesn't mean we believe ourselves responsible for having been born into this inheritance of white supremacy. Nor do we misperceive ourselves as somehow single-handedly responsible (as the white savior!) for ending the crisis of white supremacy for all times or able to accomplish such a thing.

We are clear we cannot downplay the power of racism in our white lives. But we are also clear that racism doesn't have to have the last word in our white lives either. We are clear that whiteness is not merely a fluke of biology and that, in contrast, it deeply impacts our experiences of race and our relationships and coalitions with people of color. But we also know it doesn't have to mean we remain unable to create, sustain, and be authentic in relationships across racial lines. White racial health means never downplaying how embedded in injustice whiteness is while knowing that we ourselves are not only and always bad—all at the same time.

It's a paradox. In fact, paradox is the best we can aim for. None of us, regardless of our racial identity, can be truly racially healthy as long as we live in a racist society. And for white people the paradox has the acute complexity of being related to the moral compromise and complicity being white in such a society involves us in. The goal, then, is to raise white children who are neither overdetermined nor underdetermined by being white.

Neither Underdetermined . . .

To not be underdetermined means to not downplay whiteness. It means learning and living with the recognition that being white impacts and determines a significant amount of my experience, my posture, my work, and my understanding relative to racism. I understand my white social location is always signified by the body and often accompanied by certain kinds of experiences.

In a racialized society this social location both communicates to others and is accompanied by privileges that impact so much of my life experience, experience in society, and relationships with other people. I am continuously aware that this racialization affects what and how I see, what I feel, how I understand, how I am perceived, and on and on. To not be underdetermined by one's whiteness means deep self-awareness of all of this and living in ways that are informed by this awareness.

Nor Overdetermined

To not be overdetermined means not presuming that it's impossible to challenge whiteness. Whiteness isn't stable. It's built, can be unbuilt, and thus doesn't define my soul if I actively refuse to allow it to do so. I have agency. I can learn and am able to actively stand up for justice and engage in antiracist postures. I can build skills for challenging racism in increasingly effective ways, even as a white person.

I will never get to a point that I always challenge racism perfectly. My actions against racism are always shaped by my specific white racial experience and positioning. But not being overdetermined means I am aware, nonetheless, that I am not the sum total of my mistakes and can learn to do better. I experience a deep sense of agency in terms of my ability to challenge racism and to learn and grow. All of this is what it means to not be overdetermined by my whiteness.

A healthy white identity is nurtured through experiencing the growth, freedom, and power that comes from taking antiracist stances and learning to negotiate different racial spaces. For example, one might be constantly deeply aware of one's own particular white body (not underdetermined) while also being able to connect and to navigate spaces and places that are predominantly occupied by people of color (not overdetermined). One can be comfortable in one's own skin while being positively unwilling to ever remain silent in the face of racism or accept the inevitability of white privilege.

In a society in which racial hierarchy and systemic racism are present, there is no one, fixed, healthy place. Just as one has to continually commit to good nutrition and fitness to sustain a certain level of physical health, a healthy racial identity is active, dynamic, and has to be constantly attended. What it looks like is not the same in every local context. But it is consistently marked with the clear- and wide-eyed recognition of one's own white identity and what that identity means in a racial hierarchy. This recognition is combined with a sense of agency about one's ability to meaningfully challenge and intervene in racial hierarchy and build authentic interracial relationships.

The Paradox of a Healthy White Identity

A general overview of white racial identity development theory roots our understanding of how race-conscious parenting works. At this point I want to circle back and use a story about Doritos (snack food), sharing an experience with my daughter, to give a concrete example of healthy white racial identity development.

> I was telling my two children about a racial incident their five-year-old cousin experienced at his after-school program. A child had a bag of Doritos and was letting all the kids in the class come up and smell them (yes, that delicious Doritos smell). But when T. came up, the boy stopped him and said "Not you. You can't smell them. You're Black."
>
> I wasn't surprised when my kids expressed sadness and anger after I told them about T.'s experience. But I was surprised (pleasantly) when I asked them how they would have handled the situation if they had been present. In response to that question, my white five-year-old said: "Well, I'm thinking the kid who did that was probably a white kid. If that kid was white then I think a white person needs to tell him to stop. So I would have said to that boy, 'Don't talk like that, that's mean.' "

My five-year-old daughter's reaction to her cousin's experience indicated she could see the behavior of the Dorito owner as racial behavior. She did not use the word *racist*, which was conceptually a bit beyond her at that age. But her answer made clear nonetheless that she knew the white child was not "just being mean." She recognized that this was racial meanness. This is a developmentally important and appropriate recognition.

E.'s analysis was possible because she'd had lots of conversations already not only about race and difference, but about the ways people of color are often treated. She was caught off guard at first that her own cousin was treated this way. Both she and her older sister first said "What?" with shock when I told them what happened. But she was not caught off guard in terms of recognizing the precise nature of what it was she was seeing.

It is very significant also that E. named the need for a white person to intervene in this situation. This specificity is relevant to our discussion of healthy white racial identity. She recognized this boy's behavior as a white behavior. And her response indicated she knew it was particularly important that someone attempting to be an ally (again, not her language) must intervene. This recognition indicated her self-awareness of her own whiteness too. Because she responded in this way only after being asked, "What would you do?" her response indicated she knows she is white and that her whiteness was relevant to her subsequent obligation (had she been there).

In short, my daughter did not hear this story in an underdetermined way. Her whiteness mattered and she knew it.

At the same time, she gave no indication that, because she's white and part of the perpetrator group, she was guilty. She felt responsible but not condemned. She knew she could act against whiteness in this moment. In short, she was also not overdetermined by being white.

My daughter's response indicated signs of having a sense of meaningful real agency and empowered advocacy. She saw her own ability and responsibility to act as a white person to interrupt a white racist moment. This was race-conscious analysis of the sort indicative of healthy white racial identity development.

This cannot be overemphasized. Intentional teaching about

where white people sit in this nation's racial hierarchy (and how we got there) necessarily involves teaching our children about so many bad things white people have done. It's important they learn to recognize the reality of white dominance in our society. We have to be honest about white complicity.

But it also means teaching them constantly about the possibility of agency as part of that teaching and through our modeling such. We can't be silent about white behavior, but we also must not only talk about white people doing bad stuff. We need to offer our kids alternatives they can recognize.

A Return to "I'm so glad!"

Now let's return to the first "I'm so glad" example. Despite how different it is from the Doritos story, the first example is also evidence of healthy white identity development! A child already caught in a color-blind framework would not have noticed her own whiteness, nor have felt allowed to verbalize the observation in response to what she learned at school. The recognition that white people benefit from injustice would have gone unnamed or only been insinuated.

Instead, this child's gleeful declaration—"I'm so glad we're white"—is an honest and astute assessment of her actual racial environment and her specific white positioning. She is recognizing the white privilege of not being targeted by racism.

This recognition is positive for so many reasons. First, it's evidence she hasn't already been shamed into silence about race or whiteness (something children experience early). I can imagine many white second-graders not being willing to risk making this statement to their parent. I have no doubt I would not have done so as a second-grader, especially after having been through my first-grade bathroom experience.

Second, of course this mother wants her daughter to develop a more nuanced, complex, and antiracist response than glee. But the truth is that none of us can journey toward healthy white racial identity without having wrestled with the problem of being privileged by injustice. This child is thus, as a second-grader, developmentally on her way. She is moving into pseudo-independence because she recognizes something in society is wrong and demonstrates an age-appropriate analysis that the thing that is wrong puts her on the privileged side of that harm.

Third, her ability to assess the actual racial environment and her own positioning in it offers her mother a powerful starting point from which to explore further discussion. Informed by racial identity development theory and a notion of healthy racial identity, then, a number of nurturing moves are available to this mother. In this moment a race-conscious posture will seek to support this child's assessment that white privilege exists, while also supporting the explicit recognition that, indeed, she is white. It will also help her make the connection that she can join with others to fight the injustice she just learned about.

Here are some possibilities:

- "I'm so glad you're you! And, yes, you and I are white. But what makes you glad we're white?"
  From here, in an open dialogue, there is a strong

likelihood the specific privileges and protections
her daughter had noticed or learned about will be
named. This can then easily lead to a conversation
about the mother's (and the child's) values about
fairness. "The same things that make you feel glad
you're white are actually ways of being treated
that I want for everyone: Black people, Native
Americans, and Latino/a people. So the fact that
I sometimes get treated better because I'm white
makes me kind of sad. I'm glad you are you, but
I want everyone to be treated well, not just white
people."

- From this point any number of conversations about
actions people take or ways they show they want
everyone to be treated well and fairly (from treating people fairly themselves, to standing up and
taking action when people are not being so treated)
can be pursued.

Or a different response:

- "What do you think the Black kids in your class
felt? Do you think they went home thinking they're
glad they're Black?" This conversation might help
the child cultivate identification with her African
American peers. It invites her to get specific about
how her peers (friends?) might have felt in regard
to the same things that made her conclude she was

glad to be white. And here (as above) she is likely to notice herself that she, of course, wants Black kids to also have those things too.

- This line of inquiry also might lead to a different, important dialogue. It might invite recognition of the powerful and good things her African American peers heard about themselves. A dialogue that invites reflection on the creativity and resistance that is the legacy of African Americans is also a critical race-conscious teaching that such a line of questioning makes possible. She might then intuit that very likely Black kids in her class also went home thinking, "I'm so glad we're Black!" though for very different reasons. This level of specificity is not too advanced for a second-grader. It nurtures consciousness of not just the fact of difference itself, but that diverse experiences tend to go along with our differences.

In either case, or any of the variations in between, these inquiries can be turned into a discussion not only about difference, which is where our conversations with children so often end. Instead it can be grown into a discussion about shared justice commitments across lines of racial difference, while not downplaying difference itself. It might even turn into a discussion of white people who actively participated in the civil rights movement alongside Black Americans. At least, groundwork has been laid for further conversation about this down the road, or to a mother-daughter decision to learn more together about white people who were active in the civil rights movement.

Any of these strategies affirms this child's awareness of her whiteness, rather than sublimating it the way color-blindness would, or relativizing it the way diversity-alone would. Simultaneously these strategies open up racial conversation in the interest of the child growing a deeper connection with her own values, her own experience of race, and the way her racial location connects her with others who are not white through a shared (though painful) history.

All of these responses avoid loading this moment with adult anxiety ("Oh my god, do we say that?" doesn't get the last word!), while laying groundwork for ongoing discoveries down the road.

Enabling Deeper Vision

Whatever the responses, understanding white racial identity development—both how it manifests and what healthy looks like—enables strategies and responsiveness. Such understanding supports us in envisioning our aspirations for white children in our lives. Namely, we hope to cultivate a self who is comfortable in her own skin while also being empowered as an advocate for justice. Having a vision of where we want to go helps mightily in making decisions along the way.

There are two other things that the framework of racial identity development theory make visible to parents. One is the reality that everything a child observes and experiences in his/her racial environment deeply forms identity and selfhood.

Consider the twelve-year-old whose parents have taught her color-blindness or diversity all her life. When grandma or uncle says something racist at a family gathering, she watches these same parents respond with silence. She gets confused. Maybe she develops anger toward her parents or internalizes a sense of shame. Maybe she concludes the silence is appropriate, in which case she accepts a kind of values/action cognitive dissonance.

Understanding the framework of white racial identity development cultivates recognition of how much these experiences of silence or complicity that are so common in white families impact our children. The impact goes deeper than just watching someone else model complicity in the face of racism. These experiences literally and actually shape our children's psychological development.

The second reality is that identity development theory reveals the stakes in all of our experiences. This may be overwhelming. But such a revelation is also empowering because it can enable bravery on the part of parents and other caregivers for whom decades of racial silence and tension can make such encounters difficult. Awareness of the formative power of modeling and dialogue become for us deep motivation to cultivate our own capacity. It can give us courage in the face of experiences that make us afraid.

Many parents today were raised either in families in which explicitly racist teachings were present, or in which teachings about equality were present but adults did not model antiracist interventions when racism reared its head. Many of us, thus, share a racial development journey. We have further growing to do ourselves. It's not difficult to see, for example, how a different adult response to my bathroom conversation would have generated a different set of possibilities in terms of my and my friend J.'s racial identity development path. But that would have required Ms. B. to have had a different sense of her own whiteness, to have been herself actively on a journey of healthy white racial identity.

So white racial identity development also allows us adults to think about our own identity. This is critical if we are to parent and teach white children along the lines I'm advocating. It's also a significant gift to us, then, as well. For just as conversations with our kids may surprise us in terms of what we learn from them, parenting white children in a racially conscious manner may also surprise us as we discover it's about more than our kids. We are going to get to grow in the journey too.

Takeaways

✓ "Healthy" white children are comfortable in their own skin but function appropriately in racially diverse environments. They neither ignore nor pretend not to notice the racial identities of others but do not make assumptions about people based on their race. They have strong moral commitments to interrupt and challenge racism when they witness it.

✓ Race-conscious parenting aspires to developmentally encourage children toward a healthy racial identity.

✓ Racial identity does not predetermine who we are or become, but racial identity development results from a relationship between the internal (emotions, understandings, and so on) and the external (messages, experiences with others, environment).

✓ Healthy white identity is an oxymoron in a racially unjust nation; whites can only be "healthy" to the degree that antiracist commitment and practice is at the heart of how we live.

✓ A race-conscious posture that supports healthy identity requires we acknowledge that white privilege and injustice exist, while also supporting the recognition that white people can join with others to fight injustice—and finding ways to help our kids do that.

CHAPTER 4

Do We Have to Call It Racism?

Ever since we got Mickey Mouse's greatest hits CD we'd fought song number 19, hitting the skip button the second song 18 was over. We should have known we'd lose eventually. Still, when I heard our then five-year-old singing "One little, two little, three little indians," my heart sank.[†] I waited to engage her, partly because I needed time to think it through. I wasn't sure what to say that she could understand. Partly I wanted to create gap time between her singing and my response. I knew stopping her in the act risked embarrassing her, and she'd mostly just hear she'd done something wrong. What I wanted instead was to open dialogue.

Much later in the day I started gently, "Hey, H., can I talk to you about the song you were singing earlier? The one about indians?"

[†] I'm purposely not capitalizing "indians" because the song's not about actual, real Native peoples or Indians. I think it's important that the words on the page here reflect that.

"Yes, Mama."

"I don't really want you to sing that song anymore."

"Why not?"

"You didn't do anything wrong. It's just that it's not a very nice song."

"Why not?"

From a parenting perspective that second "Why not?" is the million-dollar question. What do we say to a white five-year-old about why not? How early in their lives and how often do we use the word *racist*? What are the consequences of doing so or not?

On top of these questions, this experience brings to the surface an added difficulty. Many of us would struggle to explain clearly to another adult why we should understand images of, references to, or symbolisms about people of color, such as those in song 19, as racism. We've been shaped by public conversations about racism that are so simplistic:

"Is it racist *or not?*"

"Did that person mean to be racist *or not?*"

"Should someone be offended by that *or not?*"

The options are stark and binary. The "racist" category is under-developed. There's little room for nuance. The intention of the person doing something perceived as racist often takes center stage rather than center stage being given to questions about the impact an incident, event, or symbol may have on others.

Flat or convoluted public dialogues make it hard to have

effective and meaningful conversations about what is at stake in various racial moments. We don't get much practice. This larger context contributes to many white parents being as yet unequipped in dealing well with racialized incidents. Then, throw a five-year-old's conceptual sense of anything into this mix and we have an entirely new level of challenge. If we're not sure how to talk about and explain racism to other adults, how do we do it with kids?

Meanwhile, song 19 doesn't really say anything "bad" about Native peoples. So is it racist? Or not?

Parents of white children often look away or keep silent in the face of racism because it can be challenging to figure out how to respond. There are other reasons for our silence too. Some of us may fear we might give our child an overly negative sense of the world if we use the word *racist* too much. The word does pack quite a punch after all. Some of us might wonder if or when our children can understand what the word means. Here's an entirely different concern: I've heard parents worry that talking about racism with their child might play out in harmful ways if or when their child says something about it in front of their friends who are Black or Latino/a. These parents don't want their white kid to hurt kids of color.

> It is imperative that adults stop underestimating what children and youth perceive about race and racism.

Like so much about race-conscious parenting, there are few clear-cut right or wrong answers in response to these real challenges. There are certainly none that apply to every child in every place. But like those that emerge when we openly talk about difference with kids, to avoid directly engaging with racism doesn't reduce these risks. It merely exchanges one set of risks for others that are, frankly, far more serious in terms of long-term consequences. We can't raise children equipped to be active agents for justice, able to sustain meaningful relationships with people different from themselves, and facile, informed members of diverse, multiracial communities if we don't teach them directly and honestly about racism. So despite the reality that there's no one-size-fits-all answer, it's helpful to explore some of the possibilities and principles that can inform authentic engagements of racism by those of us seeking to raise healthy white kids.

Using the *R* Word

Many of the day-to-day direct encounters young children have with racism take place in exchanges with other kids. We might believe, then, that we can teach them to avoid racism or challenge it when they see it by simply telling them we should be nice to everyone and not be mean to anyone. We might think that teaching them to stand up for others if someone is being mean is enough. After all it's true that being nice or intervening when others are being mean are behaviors many of us teach our children. These do reflect a broader category of behaviors within which racism falls. Such an approach might avoid the sticky situations that can result once they begin to hear and then use a word like *racism*.

But there are many good reasons to use explicit and accurate language about racism. Some of these are counterintuitive. For example, we may fear our kids will use a word like *racism* in front of children of color in ways that hurt those children. But the truth is their ability to see and challenge racism is more likely to enable them to sustain meaningful friendships with those children. We might understandably fear making them overly sensitive by giving them words that seem big and scary. In fact, offering them language for the experiences they are *already having* is much more likely to cultivate their sense of agency and empowerment.

A later experience I had with H. when she was seven illustrates this latter point. That winter, my daughter was participating in a soccer camp. I sat and watched her begin to jostle with a boy while they were both in line for a drill. I overheard her say, "Hey, that's not nice! *Hey!*" She said it two or three times and was clearly upset.

In the car ride home I asked what happened. She explained he'd cut in front of her in line and told her boys should get to go first. I responded by reaffirming what she already knew: he was wrong. I told her I was pleased she'd stood up for herself. I acknowledged that it's hard to do that and said I thought it was awesome she had.

What I didn't do was use the word *sexist*. In fact, I didn't say anything about the gendered nature of his behavior. I didn't think this through carefully, but I believe my reluctance was similar to reasons some parents might avoid the word *racism*. I had a vague worry that if I emphasized the gendered nature of her

139

exchange I might make too much of it and give her a complex about dynamics between boys and girls. I didn't want her to make herself smaller or more careful somehow because she goes into situations expecting to be treated poorly because she's a girl.

Later I still felt uneasy, though, so at bedtime I circled back and asked her how she was feeling now about what'd happened. At first she told me she was fine, but then she went on to say, "That boy also said it would be embarrassing if a girl beat a boy out on the field." She was obviously still upset and definitely not fine.

At this point I could see better how small the encounter had *already* and *actually* made her feel. I could also see how little my earlier generic "good job, H." had done to help with how bad it felt. By not addressing the gender dynamics I had left her more vulnerable to internalizing gendered harm. In contrast, language to explicitly explain the experience might have supported her to process the encounter and the feelings it had elicited in her.

So I finally said, "You know what? That boy wasn't just being mean. There's actually a word for what he was being. He was being sexist."

"What does that mean?" she asked.

For the next few minutes, I tried hard to keep it really concrete and describe things in a way that might make sense to a seven-year-old. I explained that sexism against girls and women is a big problem; that it can happen at school, in families, in all the places we live and do our thing. I told her that sexism is what's happening when people say things that suggest boys are better than girls, do things to treat girls as if they aren't as valuable, or make rules that make things unfair for girls while boys get treated better.

As it turned out she hadn't even understood the boy's "embarrassing" comment until now. She'd known he was insulting her. But she didn't get that the slam had to do with her being a girl. So I explained this too. I told her that saying it would be embarrassing for a boy to get beat by a girl on the soccer field only made sense if you believed a girl couldn't be just as good an athlete as a boy. This was precisely what the boy was implying. Again, he wasn't just being mean. He was being sexist.

After all of that, I told my daughter that she's likely to have experiences like this a lot. Most important, I told her that because the boy was being sexist that when she stood up for herself, she wasn't only standing up for herself. She was standing up for all girls.

Here I had withheld information from her out of a fear I would discourage her by saying too much about how hard the world can be on girls. But instead of shrinking, the opposite happened. She became more animated. Then she shocked me with a response I'd never anticipated. "That reminds me of the woman on the bus who wouldn't give up her seat when white people told her she had to move," she said.

"You mean Rosa Parks?" I asked.

"Yes," she said. "Remember? She didn't want white people to treat Black people badly so she stood up to that bus driver."

"Yes, actually! Just like that!" I said. "You're right. Rosa

Parks was standing up against racism and standing up for all Black people when she did that. Racism is all the beliefs, behaviors, and laws in our society that harm African American people, Latino people, and all people of color."

H. and I went on to talk about Rosa Parks's courage. She pointed out to me that Parks "must have been extra courageous" because she was Black and a woman. Then we talked about how it's everyone's job to stand up—including white people (like my daughter) against racism, and boys and men against sexism.

It's clear by this point that a deep premise of race-conscious parenting is that our children can and do understand racism much earlier than adults give them credit for. Supported by evidence from social science, educators write about how imperative it is that adults stop underestimating what children and youth perceive about race and racism.[1] It's critical so we can function as supportive participants as they develop ways of being in the world that are committed to antiracism and racial justice. But it's also urgent because by not underestimating them we create opportunities for the mutual growth that dialogues and explorations engaging racism opens.[2] It's not just about children and youth. We adults who experience such dialogue stand to grow. And we stand to deepen our parent–child relationship.

My experience with H. and soccer focused on the *s* and not the *r* word—at least initially. Nonetheless, this example is an excellent illustration of educators' claims. There was such a stark contrast in the outcome between the moment I withheld truthful and specific information from H. and the moment in which I risked sharing more accurately. I nearly missed an opportunity to support her in growing an antisexism frame for her experience of the world and her place in it. It's inarguable that my daughter was ultimately better supported because I eventually listened to my gut-level sense that something still wasn't quite right and revisited the topic. The language I wasn't sure she was ready for was exactly what she needed to transform this situation from one of harm to one of empowerment.

I also nearly missed what became an opportunity for mutual growth. Our connection deepened as we explored the relationships between H.'s resistance to sexist behavior and Rosa Parks's resistance to racism. I wasn't the expert here, offering her some empowering teaching in this exchange. It wasn't one-way. On the contrary, she articulated her knowledge—and created new knowledge—through our shared dialogue. I was inspired by her. This was a mutual, two-way exchange.

This example is also excellent because even though it began about the *s* word, the *r* word did enter the room unexpectedly. In this way, my experience with H. shows the outcomes that potentially result when we've worked to cultivate a race- and justice-conscious schema with our kids. Many previous conversations about both race and gender, and stories about freedom fighters like Rosa Parks and others were already part of H.'s consciousness by the time this conversation took place. No doubt this prior context enabled her to make the connection between her own antisexist behaviors and Parks's resistance to racism, and then—even more powerfully—to the astute observation that Parks's gender and race meant she was particularly courageous. Meanwhile, this aforementioned work to create a race- and justice-conscious schema and the dialogue we pursued in this moment all cohered to support her in envisioning and recognizing herself as an agent who has the power to act in situations where "-isms" are at work.

Not every engagement is going to turn out exactly like this. Still, one of the best things we can do to support the racial health of white kids is actively invite them to surface, name, acknowledge, and inquire further into their own experiences of racism. If we break down what was going on in this situation, it can help us think about others.

First, H. was having an experience of sexism whether I decided to support her in interpreting it or not. The same is true when our children experience racism. What kids take away from such experiences has everything to do with what kind of frameworks we share with them to make sense out of such.

Second, my belief that keeping it vague and general would be less discouraging to H. than telling the hard truth about sexism was faulty. Without access to the more truthful way to analyze her experience, she was more vulnerable to a negative impact. The same is true for racism. Generic instructions to "be nice" or "interrupt it when others are being mean" don't give our kids the analysis they need in order to make them less vulnerable to internalizing racialized messages when they have day-to-day kids' encounters with racism. Generic instructions make them more likely to turn their back, be passive, or just walk away because they don't see it. Or, if they do see it, they are more likely to be overwhelmed because they have little sense of how one might realistically respond.

Finally, an unexpected but incredible outcome was that my daughter, supported with analysis, came to differently understand her abilities, role, and agency against sexism and to see herself as equipped to stand up for justice. We have every reason to anticipate similar results when we offer our children consistent support combined with language they can understand to interpret their experiences of bias and racism in the world.

This final point about agency is absolutely the most important. The central moral urgency of race-conscious parenting revolves around enabling white kids to find ways to explicitly stand up for justice and against racism. To that end, I want to come back to the concern noted above, which was articulated to me by a mother once like this:

> I worry about what to say to my second-grader about racism.
> He has lots of Black friends. I don't want him to start to treat
> them as being somehow different. I also don't want to say some-
> thing to him about racism that then he repeats to his friends in
> a way that hurts them.

It is, indeed, frightening to give young children such powerful words for fear they might end up causing hurt to their friends. This concern is legitimate. The many reasons to give our kids such language—good reasons to use the *r* word—don't eliminate the risk such hurt could happen. Yet racism is so pervasive and children use and play with race and racial images so much that it's far more likely our children will hurt their Black, Latino/a, Asian American, and other friends of color if we *don't* give them such words and analysis.

While I was writing this book, my sister shared a story about my seven-year-old nephew, T., who is Black. A few days earlier, T. had been playing with a group of kids, most of whom were white. At some point one of the kids pointed at him and said, "Your skin's the same color as poop!"

Later, my nephew told my sister what happened. "Was that girl being racist?" he asked. "Yes," my sister said. "She was trying to make you feel bad about the color of your skin. That's racism."

"I thought so," T. said. Then he continued, "And after she said that, G. [another white child on the scene] started yelling, saying to her, 'Hey, that's racist! Hey, that's racist!' "

My sister was very glad G. had intervened. More important, she could tell by the way T. reported the incident that he also saw G. as having stood up for him. Even though the experience still hurt him, T. felt good about G.'s behavior.

We need to realize that kids talk like this outside of adult earshot *all the time*. It's also worth knowing that when my sister called G.'s parents to tell them how important G.'s behavior had been, G.'s parents were a little uncomfortable. They were glad G. had done what he did. But they said they weren't exactly sure what they had done to equip him and certainly didn't feel like they somehow deserved thanks. Nonetheless, when my sister suggested they must be having some type of conversations about racism in their home, they admitted, "Yes, well, at least we're trying to. We believe it's really important."

Dialogues about kids and racism often focus on what might have been going on with the girl who used the word *poop*. But as important as it may be to understand her behavior and as much as race-conscious parenting decreases the likelihood a white child would speak in such a way, I think the far more important question is how we equip more white children to respond the way G. did. To that end it's important we recognize behavior likes G.'s is possible only if we don't shy away from big, scary words.

It may be reassuring to those of us who find ourselves daunted about how well we are going to do when we attempt to explain racism to note that G.'s parents didn't quite know what they'd done. Their uncertainty means they definitely haven't mastered a perfect set of ideas about what to do or how to do it. There's no such thing! Yet it's no surprise that behind G.'s behavior are parents who admit they are trying. Even with admitted uncertainty about how to do it, talking explicitly about racism works.

Both G. and T. came away from that painful experience with a stronger sense of possibility about white people's ability to live out antiracist behaviors. Their friendship was left intact. It became more likely to be sustained than it would have been if G. had remained a passive observer to this situation or even if he had shut down the encounter by telling the girl to stop being mean. I suspect T. left the situation less isolated and alienated than he would have had he been left to only receive comfort from his parents. I suspect G. left the situation more empowered to act against racism again next time. I know the bonds among the parents were strengthened: G.'s parents heard that their parenting choices had positively impacted T., and T.'s moms experienced parents in their community taking seriously their responsibility to equip their white children to live out solidarity with their Black son.

Partnering with Our Kids

The same educators who urge us to not underestimate children offer postures we need to take as we talk about racism with our kids. The challenge is to find the right balance between bringing our own adult values and observations into dialogue about racism with our children, without inserting ourselves as authorities as we do so. "It is important for adults to bring their own agendas and uncertainties alongside children's in these conversations," write Kimberly Chang and Rachel Conrad "but it is equally important that they do so in a way that does not override children's language and experience."[3]

One of the ways to find balance is to listen carefully and follow our children's lead. As we engage them in the work of recognizing and developing an understanding of racism and ways to act against it, our postures should be exploratory. We should stand next to them as partners. We should ask questions and offer insights about racism "as ideas to discuss rather than as right answers."[4]

We also need to anticipate that talking about racism can

raise difficult feelings. So we have to commit consciously ahead of time to stay engaged—even when it feels hard. Teachers explain that creating classrooms as spaces where antiracist learning can flourish requires giving their students explicit "permission to engage in dialogue about race and holding a lofty expectation that they will stay engaged in these conversations." When these postures are taken day after day, one moment at a time, good race talk becomes "part of the culture of dialogue" in the classroom.[5]

The same is true in our relationships with children. Teaching our children about racism doesn't mean we need to have all the explanations figured out ahead of time. We might not quite know what the right, age-appropriate lesson is in any given moment. We will often not arrive at a point of completion in any particular dialogue. We need simply commit to stay engaged with kids day after day and moment after moment. If we do, good race-talk will become part of the culture of our families.

It would have been easy for me (and I've certainly succumbed other times) to simply act in response to my panic at hearing my daughter sing song 19. I was angry at myself (and Disney) for putting her in such a position. It would have been easy to respond out of my lack of certainty about how to explain why song 19 wasn't okay, and my fear that our conversation couldn't possibly go well. But a quick response to tell my daughter to please stop singing would have ended engagement.

I didn't stay engaged at first after soccer. My own discomfort with knowing a strong "-ism" was in the room and my fear of jading my daughter caused me to artificially simplify and smooth things out. I effectively ended engagement in response to an experience that was genuinely more complex and needed open dialogue. Engagement only resulted because I eventually paid attention to a nagging doubt that I'd slowed down enough to follow her lead and a sense that I needed to create more space to talk further about what happened. Even then, I still felt nervous about how it would go.

Nerves are normal. So many of the examples I've shared in *Raising White Kids* include moments of profound discomfort. Urging parents to face head-on and proactively create more opportunities to teach our kids about racism means inviting them to accept the inevitability of discomfort. Discomfort may come from worrying about what other adults think, as we swim against a color-blind tide. It may come from worrying our attempts risk getting it so wrong we may screw up our kids in the process! It may come when our children ask questions we can't quite answer or say things that push us out of our comfort zone. But a bird's-eye, big-picture view of the positive effects and powerfully healthy outcomes of supporting our kids and being truthful can help us persist.

Here's another important outcome of staying engaged day after day and returning to dialogue about racism over and over. When we stay engaged, we teach our children to do the same. We're not trying to hand them all the right answers to racism. (What a relief!) We're modeling for them what persistence through difficult ideas and challenging encounters looks like. We're modeling a posture of being constantly interested in learning more, asking and engaging hard questions, and taking responsibility for expanding our antiracist tool kit.

When we follow our children's lead, we also have to try to respect children's language and understanding. We have to find a way to meet our kids where they are so we don't shame or embarrass them but instead support them in developing and growing. This can be tricky. Using their language and their understanding doesn't mean saying "Yes, you are right" when they say things like "I'm so glad we're white," or "Was he dark-skinned?" or sing a disparaging song about Native peoples. It does mean bringing our values and the ones we want them to embrace into our dialogues. But we need to do so while listening closely to what they say and how they say it. We need to honor and respect their processes as we walk with them as fellow travelers who stand to learn as much as they do along the way.

Finally, we need to anticipate that we will regularly experience a lack of closure.[6] Repeatedly inviting our children into dialogue and responding to them where they are while nourishing their growth is a long-term practice. If we follow our children's lead, conversations are sometimes going to end more abruptly than we had planned or wanted them to. Children's interests ebb and attentions shift suddenly.

This journey is one of supporting their development by engaging them with questions that invite more dialogue and discovery about race and racism—both in the moment and as groundwork laid for further discovery. Again, following our children's lead isn't the same thing as leaving them on their own or where they are. Sadly, we have too much white parenting in regard to race that does that already. It means giving them permission to be in process and incomplete. It also means giving ourselves permission to be incomplete and in process. We can be simultaneously deeply unsure and yet decide to engage and act anyway!

As we practice these various dispositions and postures, we will find ourselves becoming increasingly capable and facile "in the moment." But assuredly much more important, these practices also build trust, connection, and create a backdrop for future and ongoing dialogue and exchange with our children.

Back to Song 19

Following our children's lead might mean we don't use the *r* word in some moments with some kids. In fact, I ended up making a very a different decision in the conversation about song 19 than I did after soccer.

Before we go there, let's first go back to the observation that we can easily get stuck in terms of how to engage a child in a racialized moment, because we might not even know how we would explain something to another adult. One of the commitments of race-conscious parenting is to constantly develop our own analysis and abilities. In the silence that pervades white culture about race, this is practice we don't get without intentional effort. So there's something to be said for practicing breaking it down for ourselves and to others.

Perhaps you're still wondering what's wrong with song 19. Why is this childish, singsong ditty like "one little, two little" so haunting? Should we really worry about it? The reasons song 19 is racist might be less on the tip of our tongue than one might expect, given that we live in a society raging with debates over sports teams' mascots. In the gap between hearing my daughter sing this song and talking to her about it, I took some time to break this all down in my own mind.

Here's how I did that: I began to imagine that instead of "indian" we let our kids run around singing: "One little, two little, three little gay people . . ." or "One little, two little, three little Black people . . ." Can you see how much more obviously wrong this song suddenly feels?

The same reasons we can more easily access how wrong such a song would be with these substitutions than we can when the words involve Native people are the same reason this song is so wrong. Oppression against Native Americans takes many forms. Major ones are dispossession from lands and assimilation (attempts at coercively absorbing them into non-Native cultures). These specific forms of oppression have made Native peoples literally less visible in our social words than are gay or Black people. Added to this, the way we tell the story of Native peoples as a nation describes them as having existed only in the far-off past. Whether the images are romantic ones or more explicitly disparaging, they consistently imply Native peoples are a vanished and primitive people.

Psychologist Beverly Daniel Tatum reports that three- and four-year-olds asked to draw a picture of Native peoples consistently draw feathers, often include a tomahawk, and regularly include violence in the picture.[7] Surely no one sat down and said to each of these children, "Indians wear feathers and are violent." But this example indicates just how pervasive are dominant, stereotyped depictions of Native peoples in this society. Native peoples are caricatured, depicted in cartoon-like imagery. They are very rarely described as or perceived by non-Native US Americans as real and representative of an actual, contemporary, and diverse set of communities who are nothing like what the community "singing" about them sees.

The exercise of substituting *gay* or *Black* exposes what's wrong with a song that so many non-Native children are still singing. The song persists in part because we, non-Native adults, also don't think of Native peoples as real, present (as in right now, today), actual living human beings and communities. And our own ability to mentally erase Native peoples rests on the actual, concrete, and persistent structural attempts to physically erase them. This question, then, is much more complicated than "Is that song racist? Or not?" This song participates in, and thus supports and perpetuates, a larger trajectory of erasure and genocide.

> "But, Mama," she responded, "why would someone make a song they know is disrespectful?"

It was important for me to work through this in my mind before I talked to H. I needed to break down and understand more concretely for myself what was wrong with song 19.

And I ultimately said none of it to my five-year-old.

When she asked me her second "Why not?" (as in, why the song wasn't nice), I simply said, "Well, I can't exactly explain it all. But the people who that song is about—Native American people—don't like that song. They've said it's disrespectful to them. And since they've said that, and since we care about respect and kindness, I think we shouldn't sing it."

I didn't use the *r* word. I didn't talk about genocide.

I did speak specifically. I named and spoke about Native people in a way that made clear they are actual living, breathing, and real communities. In this way, my answer directly addressed some of the specific harm the song does as it perpetuates the dominant culture's vision of this group of diverse peoples as more imaginary than real. It thus countered some the specific racist perceptions of Native peoples I know my white daughter has already internalized.

I made sure Native people's agency and resistance as people was invoked: namely, Native people have said, "Don't sing this; it hurts us." Though slight, this is different in an important way than my just telling her the song was not nice to Native peoples. It was important, given the ongoing erasure, that Native peoples be named as actors. Of course, I also went on to connect what Native people have said about disrespect and harm to our family's values about showing people respect and kindness. These behaviors were already part of my daughter's sense of what is right and good. Now we made them race-specific.

Even while this particular antiracist intervention did not use the word *racism* it embodied race-conscious postures. It did not succumb to a generic or vague language ("That song just isn't nice"). It was authentic in sharing with my daughter my adult uncertainty ("I can't exactly explain it all"). It did follow my daughter's lead as I gave space for her "Why not" to take the dialogue as far as we could go. And it ended without closure being forced.

If H. had pressed me to explain what was complicated, I would have tried. But she didn't. This suggested she had enough understanding *for now* relative to her conceptual and cognitive development. But I knew (and know) we had many more conversations to have about Native peoples.

When I'm working with white people who are seeking to grow their antiracist abilities and expand their strategies I often hear them express fear (typically as a way to explain their retreat into silence) that they're not going to explain it just right and not going to be convincing. Against this backdrop of white anxiety, I love this song 19 story. It provides yet another actual experience in which the observations of social scientists and claims of teachers bear out.

Direct talk with our kids will often surprise us in ways that are so welcome and potentially wonderful. In this case, if the second "Why not?" was the million-dollar parental question, the full-blown million-dollar question came at the *end* of the exchange with my daughter. After I explained that Native people find the song disrespectful, my daughter didn't ask me why the song was disrespectful. She didn't say, "But are you sure they care? I don't mean any harm." She didn't argue, "But I want to sing that song, why shouldn't I get to when there are no Native people here?" Instead she asked me a question that revealed deeper moral and ethical insights than we often get when we try to break things down with other adults. "But, Mama," she responded, "why would someone make a song they know is disrespectful?"

In response to the many racialized messages our kids receive, a fundamental teaching we're seeking to convey is the deep respect of human beings. We choose to not participate and we seek to interrupt racism because we want to respect what actual people tell us hurts or harms them. A deep lesson exists here about simply listening to what actual people say about their own lives—and believing them.

My daughter is learning now to listen in ways that are critical to her racial development. She can't yet fully understand all the whys. But this learning is growing her ability to be able to hear her peers of color when they share the impact of racism on their lives and humanity. Modeling the posture of actually listening to Native people who have described their experience didn't require me to convince my daughter of a thing. If she doesn't see that listening posture modeled, she'll be harder to convince down the road. But at this point in her life all I had to do was give her a concrete context for what she already knew. She already knew we want to respect people. I merely drew on that knowledge to point out what she couldn't have yet known about a song 19, but which I wanted her to know.

> It's important to teach white kids not just about racism but explicitly about white people's participation in racism.

This experience was also a step along the way to further support and grow in and with my daughter a race- and justice-conscious schema that laid further groundwork even as it was incomplete. I experienced another moment that day that led me to believe that if and as we stay engaged together, H. would be able to increasingly connect the dots on her own. And, sure enough, with consistent and race-conscious dialogues along the way, two years after that discussion about the song she would do just that. Dialogue about song 19 (and many others like it) when H. was five became part of the groundwork needed for a successful dialogue when she was seven about sexism and racism and the unsurpassed courage of Rosa Parks.

Seeking Out Sheroes and Heroes

Not long ago, I was talking to another mother whose daughter is white. We were lamenting the nation's racially volatile climate. She nodded toward her four-year-old daughter and said, "I'm just really grateful she doesn't have to worry about any of this yet."

I totally get it. We parents yearn to protect our children. We want to frame things for them in positive ways. We are living in such violent, difficult times, and I want my kids to have a hopeful sense about the world and all of its possibilities. As I journey with my kids and teach them to see racism (and sexism and injustice of many kinds), I continually bump into my own fears that I'll make them cynical or cause them to see the world too negatively.

But it's worth saying explicitly that I want the parental

option to emphasize the positive to exist in equal measure for *all* children, not just mine. I understand my fellow mother's relief at imagining her daughter not having to worry about "any of this." But in the context of racism, I recognize such a disposition as possible for parents of white children in ways it is not for parents of children of color. That some kids can "stay innocent," while others cannot is part and parcel of the injustice we have to address head-on if we are going to raise healthy white kids. In a world full of racism, there is nothing innocent about innocence.

All kids—Black kids, white kids, Asian American kids, Latino/a kids—deserve parenting that takes seriously their need to develop awareness about racism while being mindful about approaches to doing so that support healthy identity. Psychologist April Harris-Britt has studied families of color and concluded, for example, that it is important that parents of children of color prepare them for racial discrimination because studies prove their kids experience it—often. But, she says, it's important to talk about discrimination "occasionally" rather than "often." "If you overfocus on [racist treatment], you give the children the message that the world is going to be hostile—you're just not valued and that's just the way the world is."[8]

Harris-Britt goes on to point out, however, that these same families teaching about discrimination are also teaching their kids to have pride in their racial identity. Such positive identity messages mitigate the risks that messages about discrimination can pose in terms of causing kids to feel unvalued or to expect hostility. For example, her research found that being "coached to be proud of their ethnic history . . . was exceedingly good for children's confidence; in one study, black children who'd heard messages of ethnic pride were more likely to engage in school and more likely to attribute their success to their effort and ability."[9] The many diverse gifts and characteristics communities of color associate with their racial identity—uniqueness, resilience, creativity, ability, community, and so many other attributes—are important for nurturing hope- and agency-filled sensibilities even while preparation for facing racial injustice is being taught.

There is a corollary discussion to be had here, then, about what these findings suggest about messages to white children about discrimination. They are being raised in a society that already locates whiteness on top and communicates many messages about white as normal or even superior. So teaching them pride in being white as a way to mitigate the risks of an overly pessimistic approach to the world would be inappropriate. White children's vulnerability is not in assuming they won't be valued in society—it's the opposite.

To precisely this end we have evidence that it's important to teach white kids not just about racism but explicitly about white people's participation in racism. To suggest that it's a good idea to be explicit about white people's participation in racism might be more surprising than my suggestion to embrace the *r* word with young children. But this actually makes a lot of sense if we take seriously the unique position of white children in a white-dominated hierarchy and the specific impact that hierarchy has on their sense of self.

One study found that stories about historical racial discrimination measurably decreased white bias. They compared white kids who learned about Jackie Robinson and who were just taught that he was the first Black player in the major leagues to white kids who were taught this but were also explicitly taught that Robinson had "been previously relegated to Negro leagues, and how he suffered taunts from white fans." The second group of white kids came away from this class with "significantly better attitudes toward blacks than those who got the neutered version." Additionally, "it also made them feel some guilt," this researcher noted. "It knocked down their glorified view of white people." Explicit teachings about racism and white perpetuation of racism decreased bias against Black people and reduced white kids' vulnerability to internalizing a sense of white superiority.[10]

At one level, the insights revealed by this study further demonstrate why we shouldn't even be tempted to take refuge in a sense of relief that my white child doesn't have to worry. It turns out an appropriate reality check about injustice and white participation in it is necessary for white kids to develop a healthy sense of racial selfhood. It's the corollary to the positive messages kids of color need about being Black or Latino/a or Native American in support of their developmentally healthy sense of racial selfhood. It's the counterpoint to the overinflated valuing of whiteness that white kids get from culture. Such research suggests we don't need to worry too much about creating in white children an overly cynical sense of the world.

At the same time, if the goal is to raise kids who are empowered to tackle racism, it stands to reason they, too, need to see themselves as having capacity to do so. We need to be authentic and teach our white kids about racism, but be mindful of doing so in ways that enable agency and not despair. We need to feed their sense of purpose and capacity in this regard. It seems to me they need to have a sense of hope and possibility; a vision of the kind of world they want to live in and a sense that their behavior and actions can help create that world.

Given the specific risks posed to white children because of how our society racializes them (for internalized superiority), we need to be especially conscious about engaging them in ways that don't reduce people of color to being seen as victims or to seeing them only in terms of discrimination. We need to be intentional to not feed into a sense of pity, charity, or "white savior-syndrome" in our kids. They must not conclude, as part of their experience of socially overvalued whiteness, they have or are the answer for people of color. Such dispositions are all developmental risks white children face, because all white US Americans face them.

Beyond the individual responses to encounters that require us to engage racist incidents and use the *r* word (or not) then, it's worth giving attention to proactive strategies that need to accompany our teaching in the bigger picture.

First, alongside our direct and honest teaching about the pervasive reality of racial injustice in the United States, which should focus on both the past and present, it's essential to emphasize the agency people of many different races have lived in response to injustice. Agency is important to mitigate what risk may exist for creating an overly cynical view of the world for our kids. It's probably even more important to buttress the risk of teaching white children about racism in ways that lead them to conclude that what it mostly means to be a person of color is to be a target or victim.

We need to offer white kids endless accounts about and relentless emphasis on the resistance and agency being lived out by people of color. One concrete and effective strategy is the regular practice of teaching our kids about past and present sheroes and heroes—people who have struggled and continue today to struggle for full freedom and equality. We shouldn't wait until our kids learn history at school. Engaging many stories with children and youth—which we can do at every age—is an essential practice. This practice not only cultivates a schema so they have access to models they can draw on for when racialized incidents happen (think H. and soccer and Rosa Parks). It also works against painting people of color as victims.

Second, we need to go far and well beyond stories about Martin Luther King Jr. and Rosa Parks. We need to expose our kids to diversity among those who have fought for freedom and equality. I found a great book for young readers about Malcolm X and gave it to my daughter when she was eight, for example. As we read it I realized what a different way of thinking about justice Malcolm X's life story presented to her than what she had mostly heard in school and even at home. Suddenly she was reading about power and dignity and the right to self-defense. These are very different messages than the

equality, integration, and peace teachings that typically sur-
round civil rights teaching.

Intentionality about diverse exposure is important for
a number of reasons. Like most adults are, our children are
already woefully undertaught about communities of color.
Dominant US culture simply doesn't lift up many accounts of
people of color's massive and myriad contributions to society
and the world. We have to choose to rigorously learn, and bring
our kids along as we do, through seeking out and engaging the
many stories that are never just handed to us in US contexts.
Making this a priority is necessary; it doesn't just happen on
its own.

In addition, historical leaders like King or Parks can easily
become, themselves, caricatures—more cartoonlike than real.
Too few images or teachings quickly devolve into stereotyping
and tropes. Communities of color need to be humanized in the
minds of our children. This is especially true as so much in
dominant white US culture presents less-than-human images
of Black people, Latino/a people, Native peoples. Constantly
learning ourselves, and teaching our kids, the diverse ways people of color have resisted and continue to resist injustice, and
going well beyond the handful of figures we learn about in
school, enables this.

Third, we also need to expose our children (at various ages)
to fiction and nonfiction stories by and about people of color
that have nothing to do with racial injustice. Author Rumaan
Alam has written about how important it is that the books
in our kids' libraries have main characters who are Black,

Latino/a, or racially diverse in other ways when the focus of the book is *not* on racial justice. As important as racial justice stories are, he writes, kids need books like *The Snowy Day*, which are simply beautiful, fun, and magic. He writes,

> We need diverse books to be sure, but those must be part of a literature that reflects our reality, books in which little black boys push one another on the swings, in which little black girls daydream about working in the zoo, in which kids of every color do what kids of every color do every day: tromp through the woods, obsess about trucks, love their parents, refuse to eat dinner. We need more books in which our kids are simply themselves, and in which that is enough.[11]

Alam, whose children are Black, said his kids have a right to such books, too; pleasurable in their own simple way.

To this I would add that white children, young and older, need such books and stories as well. Dominant white culture constantly narrates and portrays the lives of people of color in reductive ways. White kids need fictional stories about people of color that have nothing to do with racial justice. They need nonfiction stories as well about people of color whose work, journeys, and contributions to the world had nothing explicitly to do with racial justice. They need all of this for reasons of basic human growth and wholeness. They also need this to counter the risks that teaching authentically about racism may pose to suggesting the lives of people of color are meaningful primarily relative to the struggle against racism.

One final observation here. We also need to find white she-roes and heroes for our children. Doing so is not to try to build up some type of white pride. Nor is it to overstate the role white people have played or play now in fighting for racial justice. We must never overstate this. But we do need to be models ourselves and to find white models (again, both past and present), so that our kids have visions they can look toward that explicitly bring the fight for racial justice into the image or notion of what it means to be a healthy white person. Here again—our kids are going to be presented with so many images in culture that prop up stories about "good white people" who made a difference in the world by being "nice" to people of color. We need to offer our kids accounts of white people who put their own lives and work more fully on the line and in the mix for antiracism and social change.

It takes time and effort to ensure we are resourcing our kids. But there are many resources out there and they are not difficult to find. Organizations such as We Need Diverse Books or In This Together Media, which compile lists of books, and groups like Showing Up for Racial Justice, which has created forums to connect parents so they can share resources for anti-racist activist resourcing appropriate for children and youth, are just a few (I've included a list of resources like these at the back of this book). There are so many more.

The point here is this. These are proactive practices. They require us to do some new work to equip ourselves in ways we haven't been and to learn stories ourselves we didn't know before. And such practices and attention are part and parcel of the good and life-giving journey of cultivating in our white children a sense of agency and teaching them about racism in ways that both prepares and empowers them to maintain a sense of agency and possibility.

Some Working Principles and Questions

These situations in which we encounter a need to engage the *r* word are going to be as myriad and diverse as are our children and their lives. Before closing this chapter, then, I want to offer a set of questions that might be seen as a template of steps to move through or questions to ask ourselves when we experience racialized moments and seek to engage well with our children.

- Did the incident or encounter in question happen while we were alone with our kids, or is it something they reported later?
- Regardless, let's first take a deep breath.
- Next: Let's slow down and try to break it down for ourselves. Let's get clear on what we understand about why and how something is racial or racist. Let's think about what we most want to bring to the dialogue from our values as we gently engage our child in an open way.
- Let's ask ourselves these questions. What is the child saying about their self-understanding or showing that they understand in a given situation? Once we are somewhat clear about that, we can

decide what parts of their self-understanding we want to affirm and what we need to support the child in rethinking, or present as an aspiration.

- Next: What is the child saying or showing in their behavior about their understanding of other people in what they said or in what happened? And here, again, what do I want to affirm? What does the adult want to engage, support the child in rethinking, or present as an aspiration?

- Did the incident or encounter occur when others were present?

- If so, then, let's also ask: What is the impact on others or on the relationships present in the room if, or as, others (whatever their race) overheard, were addressed by, or were otherwise part of a given exchange? Sometimes we won't know for sure, and often we do have to act on our feet! But the question as we try is: What does the parent want to do, say, and/or make manifest in respect to these persons? What needs to be said to that person as well to align with the parent's own commitments to justice? What does the parent need to model for the child in terms of acknowledging others present in a given exchange?

- In regard to any incident or encounter (whether others are present or not): What response is most likely to further the conversation, be open-ended, and not assert too much (adult anxiety, for example) onto the exchange while also being explicit and direct?

- Does the exchange or experience lend itself to engaging the child in a conversation about advocacy and action in response to what transpired or what was being discussed?

Perhaps these questions feel difficult. Perhaps they feel abstract. And perhaps it will take us time to begin to sort through how to best engage these questions and respond to them, in ways that are personality-, and situation-, and age-appropriate with our children.

But the following truths simply cannot be said too many times. We get better at understanding, seeing, and responding the more we simply try to do it. We get clearer, more courageous, and more confident every time we do it despite feeling uncertain. And this most of all, what we give our children—and the children of other parents—when we engage and persist anyway cannot be captured or contained in words. It is nothing less than the gift of a future that could be different in desirable ways than the present so many of us are living in now. And that is everything.

Takeaways

✓ If there's a racial dimension to an incident among children, call it out as such; don't just say "Be nice!" or "That was mean."

✓ One of the best things we can do to support the racial health of white kids is actively invite them to name, acknowledge, and inquire further into their own experiences of racism.

✓ Basic principles: follow kids' lead, stay engaged, and assume that we stand to experience mutual growth if we practice being on a journey with them. We don't have to have all the answers—we just need to be persistent and authentic.

✓ Kids hear and use racist language and have racist incidents with one another all the time; often parents never even hear about this. We need to equip them to challenge it—which means we need to talk *explicitly* about racism.

✓ Our society already locates whiteness on top and treats white as normal, even superior. It's important to teach white kids not just about racism but explicitly about white people's participation in racism—while being mindful of doing so in ways that enable agency, not despair.

✓ Equipping white children to understand and be able to challenge racism is required if we are to create a world of flourishing for *all* children. In a world full of racism there's nothing innocent about letting white kids remain "innocent."

CHAPTER 5

Our Bodies in Racial Scripts

*During a three-day workshop I facilitated with a large group
of justice-committed Christians, folks had expressed grief and
frustration. They'd wrestled hard with the level of racial alienation, turmoil, and violence in the United States still existing
this far past the civil rights movement of the 1960s and with
what this meant for their role in justice movements. During our
last discussion, a white woman stood up. She cried as she spoke.
"I feel like such a failure. My husband and I wanted our kids'
lives to be different than ours. We intentionally put them in a
diverse school, and when they were little they had friends of
all different races. But you know what? The older they got, the
whiter their group of friends got. And we were like, 'Oh my god!
Why is this happening?' We couldn't figure out what was going
on and certainly didn't know what to do about it. And I feel like
we really just failed. For all our hopes, their worlds became as
white as ours."*

It would be difficult to overstate the frequency with which
I've heard disclosures like this. This mother's words spoke

aloud a real, complex, and sometimes painful layer of our collective racial experience. Many adults who believe in justice and equality and who yearn for sustainable multiracial community in our own lives and in the lives of our children have found our hopes dashed for reasons we sometimes can't understand.

It matters what we teach our children to think with their minds. It matters what we tell them to hold as true in their hearts. And, of course, what our minds and hearts believe informs the ways we act and move.

But race is not primarily about ideas or beliefs. In fact, one serious misunderstanding perpetuated by color-blind approaches to race is the idea that getting white people to change our views of people of color is what we should mostly be worried about. The commonsense use of *racism* in our public dialogues doubles down on this inaccurate perception. It's regularly used in ways that imply racism is primarily about individual biases.

If these perspectives on race and racism were accurate, ensuring that white children experience robustly diverse environments where they can make friendships across racial lines early in life would go a long way to eroding injustice. The logic would be impeccable.

But these perspectives on race and racism are very incomplete. Our commonsense definition of racism and our heavy use of color-blindness, turn our attention away from structural racism. That's a problem. Another big problem is that these ways of thinking cause us to dramatically overestimate the degree to which changing our (or our kids') individual views of people of different races will end racism. At the very same time they cause us to dramatically underestimate the extent to which our interracial encounters are constantly shaped and impacted by structural racism.

Race-conscious perspectives affirm a decision like the one made by this woman and her husband to intentionally seek out diversity. Sustained experience in diverse racial environments is critical for the healthy development of white children. But the experience described by this mother and so many other justice- and equality-committed parents of white children belies the ways our bodies and relationships are embedded in race. Our racialized bodies live, move, learn, work, and play, in larger racial scripts. We did not individually write these scripts. But whether we want them to or not, they directly and deeply shape our day-to-day lives—including our interracial relationships.

If having and ensuring our children have the right ideas about difference were all it took to raise healthy white kids, racial tensions and division in the United States would have been long gone by now. All the families that live in diverse communities or who have made intentional choices to put their children in diverse spaces would have raised young people whose lives and actions would have fundamentally changed our national racial landscape. That clearly hasn't happened yet.

We need to try to get this deeper dimension of race on the table. It's difficult to do, because it goes beyond language and concepts, and into bodies, habits, and space. It's even more difficult to address for the purposes of antiracist thinking and action. But we must attempt to account for this dimension of race nonetheless. As difficult as it is to get at with words, reckoning with the power of racial scripts and learning to pay attention to, recognize, and respond to the ways race is in our bodies is a key component of race-conscious parenting.

What's a Racial Script?

Whatever our unique personalities, commitments, beliefs, geographical locations, and unique individual identities, all of our lives unfold within a larger racial story. This story began long before our individual lives did. But the story continues to be written daily.

It doesn't matter who I am, for example. The day after news of yet another killing of an unarmed Black person rivets the nation, when I pass an African American person on the street *I am just another white person*. Our open national racial wounds, violence, and trauma exist—pulsing in the air—between that person and myself. These long-standing wounds mediate all initial encounters between people of different races. They often prevent anything more than a first encounter from taking place.

Racial scripts are about intergroup racial relationships and histories. They are collective. We inhabit them no matter who we are: regardless of when our ancestors migrated here, if our ancestors were forced by way of enslavement, if our ancestors were original occupants of this land, and/or if they migrated here in recent decades because conditions and crises in their country of origin were such that doing so was the only way to ensure we, their descendants, would have a chance to flourish.

Sometimes, when we get to know people across racial lines, the power of scripts becomes muted. Stereotypes that exist about people of color are debunked. The assumption that white people just don't care about the plight of Black or Latino/a people might begin to hold less sway. At the same time, racial scripts are so powerful and thick they impede our ability to get to know one another deeply. Even if we're around one another a lot—at work or school, for example—they don't go away without some type of specific (and sustained) attention to address the history of injustices and inequity in which all of our lives unfold.

On top of this, even when we do build relationships with one other across racial lines, the power of racial scripts means they can take over at any moment and negatively impact our relationships. I was talking to a pastor of a local, very multiracial church not so long ago. He was telling me about how successfully and beautifully his unusually diverse congregation engaged one another, sitting down for meals, worship, and life together week after week. They had done so for years, he said.

But as video after video rocked the nation in the months and years following Michael Brown's killing in August 2014, his church began to change. A different tenor began to manifest in people's relationships. It was more obvious there were things going unspoken. He began to realize there was a whole other level of relationship to which even this successful multiracial congregation, full of relationships that seemed authentic and meaningful, had yet to arrive. The relationships in this community were impacted by—and became more obviously impacted post-2014—the social and political environment in which they were embedded.

At this point, the congregation began to engage the vulnerable, difficult, and harder work of engaging the crisis of anti-Black police violence (slowly and with great care). They began a journey to explicitly engage the power of structural injustice and white supremacy in their lives as differently raced people. They did it together. This was a harder project and required a different kind of language and learning for white members of the church than for Latino/a and African American members. But it was only then that entirely new possibilities for and depths within relationships in the community began to be unveiled.

This story illustrates the power of racial scripts. It also illustrates the ways deeper multiracial engagement might go beyond embracing individual difference and into the harder work of collectively addressing the wounds, violence, and harm that are present in the environments in which our diverse relationships are being pursued.

Besides being larger than our individual or familial lives, or our personalities and commitments, racial scripts contain highly predictable patterns. Patterns repeat.

My white students are reluctant to discuss race. Their individual reasons for such reluctance tend to be highly predictable. But whatever those reasons, if or when they succumb to this reluctance they step into a predictable role: for their peers of color, white students perform "white disinterest" and "lack of care." These roles are part of an existing script.

Before any serious, authentic dialogue has even been tried, the air is already loaded with stories and expectations. In a classroom setting, only carefully addressing these racial scripts *before* dialogue even begins reduces the likelihood of predictable pitfalls emerging during said dialogue. For example, we have to get on the table—for everyone to see, discuss, and, we hope, understand—the reasons behind white students' reluctance to engage race. We have to get on the table the reasons behind the suspicion of students of color regarding white authenticity and frustration about white reticence. These discussions focus on the larger context in which we are coming to the table, and we have to have them before we can have good interracial race-talk itself.

Or consider interpersonal engagements across racial lines. An argument between two coworkers or a frustrating encounter between an airline agent and a customer—the content of which has nothing to do with race—can become racialized in a split second! Did that white person use that tone with me because she is actually racist? Did that Black person use that tone with me because I'm white (that is, is she assuming I'm racist)? The wounds of structural injustice, unhealed violence, and, for many of us, prior painful experiences across racial lines hover so close to the surface that any conflict can suddenly become all about race. No racial words need be spoken for this to happen.

People of color regularly describe the experience of having

their unique personalities, interests, and experiences reduced to one-dimensional stereotypes. Racial scripts function similarly. They are less about inaccurate or negative stereotypes regarding white people, however. They are more about the ways being white has put white people in a particular location in a system that is larger than we are individually, but which continues to damage and harm people of color. Our being white communicates complicity in that system long before our true character can be revealed.

We who are white might feel frustrated about the existence of racial scripts. They seem unfair. Of course we want to be responded to on the basis of our individual personalities and commitments. None of us want to be judged on prior assumptions that come out of larger histories we didn't personally control. Meanwhile, our insulation and privilege in a system of white racial hierarchy tends to give us lots of experience being given individual, benefit-of-the-doubt treatment.

But of course, people of color want to be treated as individuals too. It's rare, however, that they are able to count on such treatment because of the pervasive presence of racism.

For all of us, race is always about larger stories, group experiences and structures, and shared, inherited histories. The phenomenon of being reduced to being "just another white person" because of our location in larger histories and systems is a corollary to the endless ways people of color are constrained and contend with roles or assumptions and expectations placed on them as a result of systems of white supremacy. (White supremacy is the cause of this, not people of color. So if we don't like this, we need to challenge white supremacy.)

Structures of racism impact all of us. They impact how we see one another or expect to be seen. And they consistently mediate our relationships with one another as a result.

Racial Scripts in the Lives of Kids

Racial scripts continually shape our experiences across racial lines because much of the time we go on to play the part we are handed. Racial scripts can be disrupted—but disrupting them takes informed, intentional, and specific choices. These choices must be made over and over again, and sustained over time.

As we seek to raise healthy white children, parents must come to understand this phenomenon so we can practice reckoning with scripts' impact. If we can learn to respond to and disrupt racial scripts ourselves, we can also teach our children to see and disrupt them as well. A story from my own life gives a glimpse into a way racial scripts impact children and have long-term developmental effects.

In first grade (again with Ms. B.!), I had a good friend named M. I was white. M. was Black. We were tight. I invited M. over to spend the night at my house. After checking in at home we both thought we were a go.

When Friday came, I called my mom at work and she told me to call M.'s house to let her know when my mom would pick her up. But when I called and started to explain this to the adult female on the phone, the woman (probably M.'s mother) became incredulous. I

don't remember all of what she said, but I remember her
emphatic "M. is not sleeping over at your house."

I crumpled. I was devastated and embarrassed. I
knew I had bumped into something big and powerful.
When my mom got home from work that evening, she
found a stack of notebook paper in my room. Over
and over again, in my first-grader scrawl—more than
one hundred lines of writing by her count—were these
words: I'm sad. I'm sad. I'm sad.

All children are better off when they experience and perceive diversity as the normative state of reality. This is especially important for white children, however. Kids of color in the United States are already more likely to live lives in which they learn to relate to, and engage and work with white people. White kids, on the other hand, are being raised by white adults whose social networks are 91 percent white.[1] They are more likely to spend most of their time in contexts that are demographically mostly white. They are uniquely vulnerable to internalizing notions of being superior because of being white in a society that is a white racial hierarchy.

Experiencing diverse environments can potentially mitigate some of the perilous socializing environments white contexts pose for white children. They may become better able to function well in diverse contexts. They are more likely to create meaningful interracial relationships. My relationship with M., for example, was only possible because I was being educated in a robustly diverse setting. Remember? I was only one of six

181

> We also need to find ways to teach our children about the social conditions and wounds that impact interracial relationships.

white girls in my first-grade class. And even though it isn't guaranteed to bear out, such relationships do create more possibility that white youth will be positively impacted toward antiracist dispositions as a result of those relationships.

Acknowledging the existence and power of racial scripts is not a case against the value of diversity. On the contrary, acknowledging the existence of scripts and dealing with their impact is essential if the outcomes many parents of white kids say we want from diversity are to be realized.

Without specific work to counteract the power of racial scripts meaningful diversity simply cannot sustain itself. Children engage, imitate, and respond to adult modeling, much more than they do to what adults say. Children perceive, feel, and internalize adults' affect, energy, and behavior. They integrate these noncognitive perceptions into their sense of reality and do so at levels much deeper than they do the explicit teachings adults offer them.

As a result, diverse environments cannot fundamentally change the racial dynamics in, and experiences of, white children and children of color's lives. Children experience their friendships in the context of the same racial tensions and larger societal racial alienation that adults do.

Simply put, adults haven't figured out how to address and

reduce racial tension among ourselves. This is true at the individual or micro level—for example, in relationships across racial lines with coworkers. It's also true at the collective or macro level—for example, in the staggering racial divides in this nation measurable by any number of data sets. How could this *not* impact our children's relationships with one another? If we live in a nation, in communities, and in families in which either or both racial separation and racial tension are present, *we should expect* our children to bring this to their peer groups.

At best, the expectation that diversity alone can make our children immune from racial separation and/or tension (and sustain itself), is a result of a flawed and simplistic view of race—that difference is "only skin deep" and we merely need to teach them to not have biases against those who are different. At worst, we are thoughtlessly expecting our children to do, and solve, something we have not ourselves done or solved; and our kids have experienced us not do or solve. If we want diversity to be meaningful for white kids, then we have to model disruptions of racial scripts and have frank conversations about their existence and impact.

Letting Them in on the Story

When we see children like M. and myself in elementary school, happily playing across racial lines, who are no longer friends and sitting at racially segregated tables by middle school, we are not observing middle-school students having suddenly become racist. We are observing the symptoms and long-term effects of their having breathed in the racially complex, tense, and difficult climates in which we all live and through which all our bodies move. We are witnessing youth who have not been provided the tools to navigate these climates. Self-segregation over time is a highly predictable outcome of the racial scripts in which our children live with us.

Part of race-conscious parenting, then, is to become attentive, careful interpreters of racial scripts. We need to know how to address, redress, and defuse them. We also need to find ways to teach our children about the social conditions and wounds that impact interracial relationships. If we don't, when they experience the frustrating dynamics racial scripts create or have to navigate the tensions and hurt that multiracial spaces are often seething with (especially in schools), they are more likely to direct their frustration at people of color. They, like we, need to direct this frustration instead at the structures of injustice that generated the scripts to begin with. Our children's abilities to build and sustain meaningful interracial relationships and engage in friendship and advocacy means they must learn to navigate and capably disrupt racial scripts too. That I'm just another white person until proven otherwise means diversity in my life requires actions and behaviors that constantly attempt to *prove otherwise*.

If diversity alone is not enough, recognizing the presence of scripts reveals constructive options we can choose. Explicit conversations with our children about their experiences in diverse context are a must. We have to talk with them about the ways diversity is *hard*.

A few years ago my five-year-old nephew, who attended

a very racially diverse school, started talking about playing dodgeball at school. He announced to my sister and me, "We're not supposed to say 'Black kids against the white kids!'" My sister and I suppressed a laugh. But when we asked him if he knew *why* his teachers didn't want the kids to say that or whether the teachers had talked to the kids about why, we were troubled. "Nope!" he said.

What a perfect example of diversity having created an opportunity for explicit racial learning. Misguided as it was, the idea of Black versus white dodgeball wouldn't likely have come up in a nondiverse setting!

I suspect there was a mixture of a kind of developmental naiveté going on, combined with an emerging, conscious awareness among these kids that racial tensions exist in their school. But when teachers chose not to explore the reasons not to play racially divided dodgeball, these students were left more likely to succumb to tension-filled racial scripts as a result. These kids are going to square off as Black and white in some other way.

An added layer of irony here is that the social existence of hostility between racial groups, which exists even when nothing explicitly racist has happened, is the very reason these teachers don't want the kids to make divided dodgeball teams. What an incredible opportunity! Not only did many constructive options exist for race-conscious dialogue in this moment, but such responses would have been actual interventions in and disruptions of the scripts themselves.

I can imagine any number of interesting and important mul-

185

tiracial conversations teachers might have invited in response other than shutting down racialized dodgeball with a no.

In the immediate response, a line of questioning that would invite the more open-ended dialogue might include one or more of the following:

- "What an interesting idea. What made you think of this? What makes you interested in dividing up the teams like that?"

- "What about kids who are white but have good friends who are Black, or Black kids who have good friends who are white? What if they want to be on their friend's team?"

- "But how do we know for sure who is white and who is Black? What about students who have family members who are Black *and* white? What about students who are Latino/a or are from Vietnam? How do you think these students would feel about that kind of dodgeball? Whose team would they play for?"

- "What an interesting idea. Have you seen this way of dividing people up in other places? Are there sports teams that you've seen divide people up by race? Are there places in our city where you see only white people or only people of color? Are there places in our school where it feels like white kids and Black kids are competing against each other?" (Sidebar: I imagine this line of questioning

in particular would elicit fascinating and highly
important insights into what kids actually observe
about their communities; things teachers don't typically hear. These would open great potential.)

An outgrowth and longer-term set of dialogues and educational explorations that could follow from an open-ended,
nonshaming and non–anxiety-laden response to this incident:

- "You know, I'm uncomfortable with Black-versus-
  white dodgeball, but I want to talk about why and
  share some stories about my reasons." Here would
  be a great opportunity to engage in some historical
  or contemporary stories about racial injustice and
  hostility, in which both white perpetration and people of color resistance was featured. This could be
  shared as one reason for the teacher's discomfort
  about racial teams and as a way to ask students
  about their values. In this context, stories in which
  some white people broke ranks and engaged in
  justice-work with people of color would be important as well. Such storytelling would educate kids
  about why racially divided dodgeball seems dangerous and invite students into moral visioning
  about what kind of world they want. It would
  almost surely get them talking about their relationships with one another.
- "You had such an interesting idea when you

wanted to divide up to play white kids versus Black
kids in dodgeball. And we talked about why the
teachers didn't think that was a good idea. But
it made me wonder—is Black kids against white
kids sort of like making girl lines and boy lines at
school? What do you think about that? Maybe we
shouldn't do that either?" Or "Is playing Black kids
against white kids the same thing as if we played
boys against girls, or students against teachers in a
game? What's the same about it? What's different?"

- "You had such an interesting idea when you
wanted to divide up to play white kids versus Black
kids in dodgeball. And we talked about why the
teachers didn't think that was a good idea. Do
you think if we let you play dodgeball that way it
would be harder for white kids to stay friends with
Black kids, and Latino/a kids with white kids?"

I wish I had been there to be in on such a conversation.
I'd bet that incredibly nuanced, powerful, and unexpected dialogues would have opened up among these children and their
teachers if some of these questions had been asked. And, again,
the responses they elicited could become routes for all kinds of
further race- and justice-conscious explorations.

As with other race-conscious responses, these questions
get at what's being communicated by the kids about their self-
understanding and their understanding of others. They attempt
to humanize and get specific about the individual people who

are being grouped into larger categories (destabilizing these categories a bit too). They resist imposing adult anxiety, but engage in a redirection that is open-ended and joins alongside these kids in their reasoning process. And by taking these types of postures, these lines of inquiry lay groundwork for ongoing explicit dialogue about race, difference, and interracial relationships and community. They do the important work of bringing our collective histories and contemporary experiences into the room for shared investigation.

Meanwhile such collective dialogue would have also, in and of itself, been a disruption of the racial scripts that this dodgeball moment suggests some students were becoming aware of on a conscious level. It would have countered the scripts' power by making them visible to the students and modeling "no fear" in talking about them. It would have put on the table for the kids to see (and thus develop language to talk about and better understand) the larger contexts in which their relationships exist. This is very much along the lines of needing to have a discussion with my college students about why talking about race is hard, prior to actually having the racial discussion itself.

If we become aware of how pervasive racial scripts are, we will stop overestimating what diversity alone can be expected to accomplish. More important, we can become more prepared to create constructive opportunities out of the moments in which our kids experience and encounter these larger inherited racial dynamics in diverse contexts and interracial encounters and exchanges.

Relationships Can Always Get Racial

I now know, of course, that my first-grade friend M. and I had been set up. Not by anyone on purpose. But we were playing out a racial script. In this case, this script had more to do with social structures than it did with tension in our friendship because neither of us had internalized larger, collective racial tensions—yet.

We kids had made the sleepover plan. I don't think my mother ever actually spoke to M.'s mother directly, though I can't be sure. Now before you conclude *this* was the obvious reason the sleepover didn't happen, more relevant than race having been in the mix, please remember that parenting culture today makes that detail of this story far more unusual now than it was back in the mid-1970s. As hard to imagine as it may be for parents now (including myself!), in elementary school I had sleepovers all the time with white kids whose parents had never met my parents!

But my family lived in a part of Denver, Colorado, that was geographically far removed from M.'s. We lived across town in a mostly white neighborhood. She lived in a mostly Latino/a and Black neighborhood. The city was very segregated. Looking back, I think, *Of course! What African American mother would possibly think it safe to let her child go sleep over at the home of a white kid and family she'd never met? Let alone allow her daughter to be picked up by a virtual stranger and driven across town.*

There were many layers to this experience. Among the most important were the adult postures and structural realities:

her family's understandable suspicion, my mother's unaware-
ness that such suspicion should be expected, and deep-seated
residential housing segregation. Our lives were worlds apart in
ways I did not see at all before this incident, and for reasons I
didn't understand for years afterward. A structural address of
injustice—a system of busing to create racial integration—was
the only reason our friendships could come into existence at
all. But the remaining social scripts in which we still lived made
it virtually impossible for the diversity we were immersed in at
school to sustain itself or be meaningful for the long haul.

There were various and diverse types of failures by the
adults (parents, teachers, school board legislators, and on and
on) under whose watch this childhood relationship took root.
As a result of these a deeply important friendship between M.
and myself became utterly racial that Friday. I have no memory
of M. after this point in first grade. I viscerally remember the
feeling of being so stunned by having my high, happy hopes
abruptly dashed, and knowing beyond a shadow of a doubt
that something deeper and bigger than "not this time" was
afoot, that the pain stayed with me far longer than it took me
to write *I'm sad* one hundred times. I have no idea what M.
thought, felt, or experienced. Of course, I experienced no adult
support afterward to help me process the racial dimensions of
this incident. I don't know if M. did or not.

This is just one story of so many. It's no surprise my diverse
school experience would, by seventh grade, manifest as self-
segregated groups of children wandering the halls. My own
friend group became almost exclusively white. And this was

without even accounting for the ways racial tracking of students within the school through accelerated courses and programs for gifted and talented further engineered our alienations.

Proactive, race-conscious attention to the various layers of our children's social realities—from what they learn about difference, equality, history, and so on to the kind of environments in which we choose to place them—creates a larger framework within which the impact of racial scripts stand to be significantly reduced. Prior race-conscious parenting practices might have altered some of what transpired between M. and me. We might have persisted further in our friendship if racial self-awareness and facility had been more developed in my own life.

But even within a race-conscious framework it's crucial that parents cultivate understanding of the specific ways structures and larger collective narratives shape the racial lives of the communities of which our children are a part. We have to respond to these specifically. In my story, much more was required than simply better equipping M. or me.

For example, at minimum, there needed to be a clear-eyed appreciation of the barriers posed by a long drive from one side of town to a mostly white part and to the home of an unknown white family. In this context a white parent must go above and beyond the behaviors a parent might otherwise embody if the child being invited to a sleepover is also white. This might mean the white parent reaching out with a phone call asking or offering to come by and meet the friend of color's family. Perhaps it might mean asking first about meeting up to play at a playground near that child's house, in *their* neighborhood.

Going further, parents of white children who value the diversity their kids experience at school need to also commit proactively to full participation in all matters pertaining to the needs and concerns of Black and Latino/a families at

> The bodily dimensions of race can create racial dynamics in collective spaces without words ever having to be spoken.

the school. One way to disrupt the power of scripts is to find ways to embody visible antiracist commitments long before a sleepover invitation is extended. Sustained, public commitment as white parents can challenge, to a degree, the racial scripts that otherwise impact our children in specific contexts. Meaningful, interracial relationships at our kids' schools stand a much greater chance of being strong and sustainable to the extent cohorts of white parents are active, visible antiracist allies to parents and children of color at school.

Authentic, meaningful, and powerful interracial relationships can be built. They do exist. With sustained and serious effort over time we can slowly rewrite these scripts if we so choose. And a commitment to raising healthy white children is a commitment to figuring out and engaging in concrete practices to do precisely that.

Race Is in Our Bodies

Chuck E. Cheese was packed during my daughter's friend's birthday party. A large group of young African

American kids (ages in the range of, perhaps, seven to eleven), who seemed to be part of an extended family, were running around enjoying themselves immensely. Fewer adults were present with these children than there were other groups (mostly white people) in the space.

Before long I began to experience in my body that the dynamics in the space were feeling racial. I noticed white adults giving quick glances toward this group of children. The glances weren't hostile. But they definitely had a vibe. The kids were being pretty loud and they were running—a little overwhelming given how crowded the place was. But there was more: a discernible physical avoidance of these kids by the white adults in the space that was really unnatural. I also noticed the kids never made eye contact with the white adults or white kids in the space and vice versa. Avoidance was everywhere, even when someone might accidentally bump into someone else; a case in which eye contact would be a pretty typical response.

It was like each respective group of folks was closed off inside a racial bubble. You didn't see it exactly. No one would have named it. But I am betting most of us could feel it.

It's difficult to describe this experience in words. But it's akin to this: imagine you as a white person walking into a room of twenty-five Black people. You feel race in your body.

And I know, because I have heard people of color say it many times, when you as a Latino/o person or African American person walk into a room of twenty-five white people you feel it. We feel race. Race is in our bodies.

I was feeling race that afternoon and it didn't feel good. The feel was markedly different than it would have been if the kids running around in a group had been the same race (white) as the majority, in which case the white adults wouldn't have been so avoidant. I was sure these children had to be sensing the racial vibe too.

Then, at one point, just as I stepped up to help my daughter with a game, a boy (perhaps about nine) from this group stepped up at exactly the same time. Consistent with the larger dynamic in the room, he didn't look at either me or my daughter, even though we were going to have to negotiate who was going to go first, a negotiation that would often happen by way of some type of body language and eye contact.

This child happened to have a great haircut with amazing designs shaved into his hair. In the moment in which it wasn't clear whether he or my daughter was going to play the game first, I stopped him and said, "Hey! I totally love your haircut." For a microsecond he paused and looked startled. Then, as my words sank in, he broke into a huge smile. "Thanks!" he said. After that we both made person-to-person eye contact and smiled.

Then this: for the next hour, this child and several

195

of the kids he was with chased my daughter and me
around Chuck E. Cheese. They came up to my daughter
over and over, shoving tickets in my daughter's hands
every time they won a game. Handfuls. Hundreds. It
was particularly sweet because she was so much younger
than they were; she was beaming from the attention and
generosity of older kids. Even as we were trying to leave
after we exchanged her undeserved, unearned stacks of
tickets for more toys than she could have ever dreamed
to hope for, they came up to her again—more tickets.

This was the only interracial interaction I saw tran-
spire at Chuck E. Cheese the entire afternoon.

This experience illustrates another dimension of race. It
pertains to the larger scripts in which our lives unfold, but
goes deeper still because it brings into focus the literal, physical, bodily dimensions of race. Race is in the way we move
and hold our bodies in shared spaces. The bodily dimensions
of race can create racial dynamics in collective spaces without
words ever having to be spoken. And interracial relating happens physically, too, in such contexts. Again, without words
needing to be spoken, the ways our bodies relate increases or
reduces racial tensions or hostility, or increases or reduces connection and engagement. Meanwhile, our children all experience all of these feels.

If it's difficult to write about racial scripts, it's even more difficult to write about race within and lived out through bodies.
This experiential, bodily dimension is that much more beyond

words. It pertains, in part, to a shared, collective awareness of social racial tensions, suspicions, and sometimes animosities—because many of us know, in some way, that we've all been handed a role in a larger play.

I felt like I was breaking a real taboo when I spoke to that young boy. This wasn't because I feel uncomfortable engaging young children or African American people. It wasn't about me or him. It was about the creation of spatial (and racial) dynamics at a collective level.

The racial dynamic at Chuck E. Cheese that day was palpable and so much bigger than this child or me. I am convinced he felt it as much as I did. The dynamic, too, was intensified by the restaurant's location in West Des Moines, Iowa—a suburb of a very racially segregated Des Moines, Iowa, which lies at the heart of a state that is demographically very, very white.

Racial dynamics manifest in any place or space. But the way they communicate or the ways we read them is informed by local contexts. How I experienced and read what was happening at Chuck E. Cheese was different than what I would have read had we been in Brooklyn, New York. The bodily dimensions of race are always context specific.

Because of his initial response, it seemed to me this child anticipated some sort of correction as he heard me begin to speak. His subsequent smile and exuberant reaction seemed to suggest our exchange was somehow unanticipated and, ultimately, welcome. I can't know for sure of course. But, really, what nine-year-old voluntarily gives up hundreds of coveted Chuck E. Cheese tickets?

My hypothesis is that race and racial divides—in this case, the unexpected crossing of a divide—had everything to do with the interactions that unfolded between this child (and his friends) and myself and my daughter. For my part, I *felt* the relief and release of not staying inside my racial bubble in that highly racially divided space.

Researchers have attempted to study the ways that racial perceptions, scripts (my word, not theirs), and divides show up in our bodies and how we hold our bodies in space. These have something to say about what *might* have been going on at Chuck E. Cheese.

> Even if we have all our ideas, beliefs, and thoughts correct, as white people, our bodies will give us away every time.

For example, social scientists Phillip Atiba Goff, Claude Steele, and Paul G. Davies attempted to understand how racial inequality has continued at the same level for the last sixty years in our society, when studies find "a consistent decline in the expression of anti-Black racial attitudes."[2] Looking for mechanisms that perpetuate racial behaviors, even when conscious bias is absent, these researchers conducted a study in which they measured how far away white people placed their bodies from Black people in various scenarios where they were supposed to have a one-on-one conversation. They found that in situations in which white people were afraid their engagement across racial lines put them at risk of being perceived as racist, they would literally sit farther away from African Americans.[3]

It's possible something like this could have been going on, at least for some of the white people at Chuck E. Cheese. So much of the engagement there might have involved negotiations over which kid was going to get in line first for skeeball, or asking running ten-year-olds to be a bit more careful around the two-year-olds in a crowded space. Perhaps there was fear that engaging African American children in these ways might have been interpreted as racially biased somehow. So white adults in the room dramatically opted to disengage completely. Don't look or make eye contact. It's too loaded!

There are other possibilities too. Philosopher Shannon Sullivan writes about the ways our ongoing habits and practices over time literally make up the physicality of our bodies—the feel, movements, perceptions. She explains this to point out the ways that white privilege does not just impact white people's way of thinking, but our ways of "bodying."[4] Bodying, the physical correlate to thinking, is produced by the ongoing experience of being white in a white racial hierarchy. We end up bodying whiteness because of the cumulative effect of what we do in spaces, how we are treated in and navigate spaces, what we do day in and day out—which creates habits, which creates environments, which "bodys" us again.

Sullivan writes, for example,

> The books that a person reads, the films that she sees,
> the histories that she studies, the people with whom
> she socializes, the neighborhoods in which she lives, the
> social and political work to which she contributes—all

of these are environments that help shape a person's
habits and on which a person can have some impact.[5]

In terms of Chuck E. Cheese, a different possibility than
a fear of being perceived as racist might also be plausible.
Sullivan's line of inquiry suggests it might have been that the
odd "racial bubble" effect was a product of white people being
bodied through endless participation in radically nondiverse—
meaning, white—spaces. Such bodily formation could easily
result in white people in a restaurant experiencing an aversion
to physical interaction with a small but highly visible group of
Black children.

For many reasons, including the fact that this is all so beyond
words, it's impossible to unequivocally know for sure what was
going at Chuck E. Cheese or what might be going on in other
situations like it. It's also risky to make claims that are too certain. On top of this, because I can only write of my interpretation of this experience, I risk projecting my perceptions onto
this child and his experience in a manner that disrespects him by
being presumptuous about how much I can know, or that could
be flat-out wrong. (Each of these caveats are also relevant to my
writing about M. and our failed slumber party, as well.)

Having said all of that, I don't think I'm wrong. And writing
to illuminate experiences like this is worth the risk because this
dimension of race is so important. It has such a major impact
on our racial learning. Even if we have all our ideas, beliefs, and
thoughts correct, as white people, our bodies will give us away
every time. The way race is in our bodies, the way we respond to

the feel of race and physically show up in interracial encounters can either disrupt racial alienation and division, or it can make them worse. Body language, eye contact, and nonlingual communications create, sustain, and/or disrupt racial dynamics when we are in a collective, group space.

Parents of white children need to tune into this dimension of race. Children learn to feel race and *stay in their place in racialized, divided spaces*. They, like we, experience race in their bodies and learn to

> We need to seek out spaces in which our children can experience being a demographic minority.

hold, use, and move their bodies in certain ways depending on different contexts. Recognizing this is an essential dimension of responsive race-conscious parenting. We must teach to this dimension of racial experience with as much attention and intention as we do the verbal, analytical dimensions of race.

For example, our children are deeply impacted if they primarily experience deeply segregated or uniracial social spaces. The older they get, the more they will palpably feel out of synch or awkward if or when they are put in situations in which robust racial differences are present. This is not because of beliefs. It is because of feels. Ask any young person of color who spends time in both worlds—mostly Black or brown, or mostly white. They will tell you that they feel different in their bodies, spirits, and emotions in these distinct spaces. This is the case even if the white people in the white space are the nicest people in the world.

The inverse is true. Drop a white child who has been equipped repeatedly with the most stalwart teachings and beliefs about racial justice and equality into a self-segregated seventh-grade lunchroom situation. That child is almost certainly not going to walk up and sit down at a table of Black children.

We have to constantly model different and disruptive inter-racial behaviors in contexts in which the unspoken but palpable collective experience of race is to stay within our racial bubble. I wasn't thinking consciously about this that day at Chuck E. Cheese. But I was very in tune with my own discomfort at the racial divides in the room.

There is no conversation I can imagine having had with my five-year-old that day to talk with her about what she was experiencing; none that could have accessibly explained to her the racial dynamics that were afoot. No verbal teaching would have prevented her from internalizing the racial divides that we were all *bodying* that day.

But it didn't take words. She observed and then, as a result of the generosity of this nine-year-old and his friends, *experientially participated in the disruption* of embodied racial division. She did not consciously recognize that this is what she observed and then participated in. But this experience still bodied her in some tiny but important way. For a five-year-old, that was developmentally significant.

So What Do We Look For?

We can become conscious about our own bodies and what we feel and then, in response, what we do with them in spaces.

And understanding that race is in our bodies allows us to make conscious choices. Where we spend our time and where we ensure that our children spend time matters. We can respond to the dashed hopes of the mother who tried diversity by making choices that act in response to racial scripts and the collective bodily dimensions of race. This is necessary for our hopes to become closer to realized.

There's no easy or abstract set of recommended practices that can be made about how to do this *in every context*. It's community- and location-specific, because it's about the concrete. I know some of what it looks like in Des Moines, Iowa. But we have to each actively figure out what it can mean where we live.

Still, I'm going to risk raising broad principles behind this dimension anyway. Despite the reality that it can be difficult in some geographical contexts, especially because of deep-seated segregation, nurturing healthy white children means we need to seek out spaces in which our children can experience being a demographic minority. Diversity is important. But given the power of white dominance to effect the bodily dimensions being described here, diverse racial experiences need to go well beyond ensuring our kids experience environments in which there is a relative racial balance or a healthy pluralist mix of difference.

Anna Olson, the mother of two white children, describes the formative impact of experiences in which white children are de-centered as she reflects on her own commitment to race- and justice-conscious parenting.

As a white parent committed to resisting racism, what do I want for my kids?

I want my kids to know how to be the only white person in the room.

I want them to know how to do this gracefully and without calling undue attention to themselves. I want them to know how to listen and observe and be a part of the action without feeling the need to dominate. . . .

My oldest daughter was, for a good part of her elementary school experience, the only white kid in the room. I could walk onto the campus of 900 students, and total strangers would direct me to my kid.

It wasn't always an easy experience for her. She felt different. Other people pointed out, sometimes rudely, that she was different. For a while, in her imaginative play, she used a pretend last name that reflected one of the dominant ethnicities in the school. She wanted black hair. When she brought hummus for lunch, other kids asked if it was "poo." . . .

What I see now is that when my daughter talks about race and culture, she gets things that many white adults struggle to grasp. She observes and has compassion for cultural differences that go way deeper than food and language, like the fact that the white kids in her middle school classes are quick to participate out loud, while other equally smart kids sometimes hang back and are judged to be less engaged. She identifies cultural bias on standardized tests (such as a vocabulary question that stumped an immigrant friend who had never had reason

to know the difference between cul-de-sac, à la carte, and
à la mode). When a person of color talks about feeling
left out or being made fun of or treated differently, she
never questions the truth of that experience, or that it
hurts. And she knows without a doubt that there is a very
real world of experience within communities and families
that include no white people at all.[6]

Olson goes on to say that in the wake of changing school patterns in Los Angeles where she lives, her younger daughter will be in a multiethnic school with more children of similar backgrounds to herself than was her older daughter. So, she says, as a parent she will have to be intentional to make sure her younger child has experiences being "outside the center."

Many of us don't have the option to ensure that our children experience school as one of six white girls in first grade or as the only one in a school of nine hundred. But recognizing bodily racial learning adds clarity about reasons to prioritize commitments about how we spend our time and in what places.

In virtually any community, however removed these may be from white awareness, people of color–led organizations and institutions exist. As parents, we need to find appropriate routes to participate in and to have our kids participate in such spaces—*if (and only if) such participation is welcome.* Sustained and ongoing participation in communities and contexts in which people of color are not only the majority but are also the leadership is a practice that deserves to be prioritized.

I have to name and highlight the real risk of making such

a suggestion. People of color, communities of color, and people of color spaces are not there for the sake of our educating our white children. This bears repeating: I'm not suggesting parents use people of color and their organizations to teach a racial lesson. White people often approach people of color in this way. I'm also not suggesting white people fall into the racist trap of trying to go "find a Black friend." This is another way of seeing people of color that is reductive and uses people to our own white ends.

But I am saying that we must consciously realize that deep segregation and division mean white people are all already racially formed and bodied by race and racism. And only through conscious choices to desegregate our lives can we learn *different* ways of bodying. Our white children also bodily learn race through the status quo ways that racial segregation and division shape their racial lives day in and day out. We have to intentionally prioritize the activity of de-centering ourselves and our children.

But, again, we only do that in spaces where people of color welcome white presence. Meanwhile, just like it's difficult to write about these dimensions of race at all, it's difficult to describe (but worth trying) the postures and dispositions we need to take if or as we engage in such spaces. For example, we actually have to decide we are engaging because we have much to learn and genuinely want to participate with humility and openness. We have to show up with a depth of commitment to stay in a sustained and reliable manner, living out a consistency of presence. We have to constantly pay attention to make sure we are taking postures that de-center ourselves—and modeling for our kids what this looks like. Olson's description of what she wants her child to know how to do describes this very well, I think.

What this looks like if one joins a faith community different from one's own is different than what it looks like if one joins (in a posture of supportive solidarity) an activist or advocacy group that is people of color–led. It's different than what it looks like if one joins some sort of community center program or other kind of collective, social gathering.

There's no way for me to write out a list of works in the abstract that makes sense in the various contexts in which we all live. It's worth adding here, too, that when we talk about desegregating our lives there are other practices we need to commit to in addition to engaging in physical spaces that are demographically predominantly people of color and people of color–led. Not only are these practices possible for those of us who live in places where there may be very few people of color. Such practices also better equip us to be humble and respectful if or when we are physically in such spaces.

For example, what kind of media do we consistently listen to? Which public thinkers do we follow online to give us commentary on the day's events? What authors do we read and how often? The daily habit of engaging the voices, perspectives, and productions of people of color (in media, art, literature, news, scholarship of many different kinds) impacts not just what we think. It potentially changes what we feel in the world as we move through it after being shaped and informed by such engagement.

Again, there's no precise *to do* list. But the takeaway point is this. The racial scripts we all live in and the bodily dimensions of race that grow out of our daily habits, engagements in space and place, and interactions with other people, are a central aspect of racial knowledge and racial development. The normalcy of racial segregation requires active attempts to overcome the ways whiteness and white racial hierarchy "teach" us and our children. The empowering insight about our bodies in racial scripts is that it raises the recognition that what we do with our bodies, and the choices we make about this daily activity, shapes and forms our racial selfhood. We can exert a great deal of decision-making power about what we do day-to-day with our bodies: about the books, the films, the histories studied, the socializing we pursue, the neighborhoods in which we live, the social and political work to which we engage and contribute to. To repeat Sullivan, "all of these are environments that help shape a person's habits and on which a person can have some impact."[7]

What are the practices in your context that you can take? How are you bringing these into the lives of your children and bringing your children into these practices? When are you aware of what your body is doing and saying that goes along with prewritten scripts? And when and how can you decide to publicly interrupt and challenge the racial scripts in which we all live to change—even if just for a moment—the role that "white people always play"? These questions are difficult but life-giving. And our responses to them in the lives of our children have everything to do with the future that they will be physically part of creating.

Takeaways

✓ If ensuring our children have the *right ideas* were all it took to raise healthy white kids, racial tensions and division in the United States would have been long gone by now. But long-established racial scripts keep us divided.

✓ Racial scripts are about collective, intergroup racial relationships and histories that impact our individual relationships in the present. These long-standing patterns mediate all initial encounters between people of different races— even kids.

✓ Interracial relationships among kids are impacted by larger social structures they live in, so if we want diversity to succeed we need to actively support them in recognizing scripts and taking action for justice to decrease their power.

✓ We feel and live race in our bodies (think: body language), not just in our minds and in words; and these bodily dimensions of race are always context and location specific. Even if we have all our ideas, beliefs, and thoughts correct, our bodies will give us away every time—and will either create connection or make it worse.

✓ Despite the reality that it can be difficult, nurturing healthy white children means we need to seek out spaces in which our children can experience being a demographic minority, remembering to *determine if such participation is welcome*, and to participate with humility and openness.

✓ The daily habit of engaging the voices, perspectives, and productions of people of color (in media, art, literature, news, scholarship of many different kinds) impacts not just what we think. It potentially changes what we feel in the world as we move through it after being shaped and informed by such engagement.

CHAPTER 6

Diversity Is Confusing!

"P. [white, age ten] came home today and started telling me about an incident at school. I never really could figure out quite what had happened. But it had something to do with her asking someone to pass her a brown crayon for a picture she was drawing. After that some of the kids in her class told her that because she wanted a brown crayon she was 'racist.' I kept trying to understand what had happened and then she looked at me—so distressed—and said: 'Mom, am I racist?'"

It's not uncommon for white children and youth to manifest confusion, even some anxiety, as they get older and become more conceptually aware of racism, diversity, white privilege, and other notions pertaining to race. Increasingly complex feelings emerge as they develop beyond glee ("I'm so glad we're white") or relief ("I'm white, so I'm safe!"). More challenging responses result as they start to recognize racial tensions or encounter racist discourse in their friend groups. More intellectually complicated ideas begin to be explored as they hear other young people describe things or people as racist.

In the context of a widespread cultural narrative that says, "Even if we have a long way to go, things are getting better," it's easy to forget that race and racism are no less confusing or difficult for our children as they are, or have been, for us. This may be as true for kids being raised in homes where race-conscious parenting is pursued from the beginning as it is for kids whose parents step into race-conscious approaches after they're a bit older. Whatever was happening in this school experience, P.'s distress makes sense!

The confusion P. articulated has to do, in part, with not yet having developed a conceptually full understanding of racism. This is understandable. She's only ten. Meanwhile, quips like "You're so racist!" or "That's so racist!" have become quite common in youth culture. Without yet having conceptual clarity, children and teenagers in contemporary US contexts hear the word *racist* thrown around constantly among their peers. A genuine lack of conceptual clarity, compounded by the likely possibility this word is bandied about at school, are the suspects behind P.'s distress.

Are White Kids Racist?

Racism is typically used in our society to refer to biases and stereotypes. But separate from this, unjust structures and systems exist beyond individual beliefs and biases. These systems are also racist. So one could, in theory, be unbiased and antiracist in one's commitments and yet still be part of and benefit from our unjust system. (This is, of course, only in theory. Breathing in racist "smog" actually makes it impossible to be unbiased.) Does that make him or her racist? Or is it only the system that is racist?

At the same time, even though individual perceptions are distinct from structures, these are deeply interconnected. Racist cultures build up around such structures. So being white and socialized in unjust racist systems increases the likelihood that white people internalize and act out racism—bias against people of color and false notions of white superiority.

Notice all the different uses of racist/racism in that last sentence. There are so many nuances and layers here. The frequency with which such nuanced and distinct meanings of racism are interchanged or conflated can be confusing for adults. Imagine how much more confusing for children.

Racism is so fraught and our various social contexts full of so much racial tension. As a result, when white children and youth experience confusion it's easy for them to respond by just disengaging. I regularly point out to my college students that most of us have had few to no experiences with good, productive dialogues about race—while many of us have had

"I know I'm white so is that the same thing as being racist?"

experience with hurtful dialogues. A fundamental practice of race-conscious parenting, then, is to aid our children to grow their understanding and clarity about these distinct dimensions of racism. We need to support them in working through concepts related to race, so they are more prepared when they encounter race and racism talk among their peers. Enabling our kids to develop clarity is one way to cultivate their resilience in the face of racially challenging environments and a whole lot of race-talk in the public square that, frankly, isn't very good or particularly well informed.

The story above indicates something more specific and difficult, however, that also needs attention. P. seems worried there is something negative about who she actually *is*. Her question to her mom has to do with some sort of awareness that racism is bad, has to do with white people, and perhaps even to do with her own whiteness. She doesn't seem sure what this thing is or what the connections are. But her encounter with her peers has brought real anxiety to the surface.

P. seems to really be saying something like this: "Mom, am I racist [because I know I'm white so is that the same thing as being racist]?" Subtext: ["I really, really, really hope not because I know racism's really bad and I don't even know what I'm doing wrong."]

As they age, white youth developing race-consciousness may, indeed, begin to have conflicted experiences about how their own white identity pertains to their relationship to racism. This is to be expected.

White people do face unique challenges when it comes to the meaning of our racial identity in a world of racism. These challenges can actually be exacerbated by exposure to diversity, and may become more acute as our children develop intellectual awareness of the power of race in their lives. How does a young person begin to navigate the difficult puzzle of living in a hierarchy that unjustly privileges her because she's white (but wanting to be a "good" person)? Raising healthy white children requires us to understand the anxieties these challenges evoke so we can both anticipate and respond to them in our parenting.

When I reacted to my daughter after the protest ("Yes, we're white, but we want fairness for everyone"), for example, I did not explore with her the meaning of white privilege for who she and I are as people. In that moment and stage of her development, a focus on fairness, safety, and equity for others was the primary point. But the confusing feelings caused by an increasing awareness of white privilege will return (and has)— and has to be addressed. In moments like the one this mother experienced with her daughter P., there's a need to directly support white children in scrutinizing their own embodiment. We need to talk with them about how they feel about being white, what it does or does not have to do with "being racist," and even about how confusing diversity can be for them, given their whiteness. These more complex aspects of white racial development, which can be supported by clarifying teachings about racism, are the focus of this chapter.

"White" Is a Vexed Location

In the 1990s sociologist Mary Bucholtz spent hours and hours in conversation with students at a racially diverse high school in California. She was interested in understanding the "imaginary lines of race." Race is a construction, after all. But this construction has real consequences in the lives of youth.

Specifically, Bucholtz wanted to know how white youth experienced "being white" in the context of larger social dialogues about race and difference. In this case, a study conducted in a high school where a commitment to multiculturalism was central to the curriculum was a perfect way to get at this question.[1]

Bucholtz asked students to identify their age, sex/gender, grade, and race/ethnicity at the start of every interview. On their face, these seem to be pretty straightforward questions.

But something fascinating happened. In almost every case, white students couldn't or wouldn't answer this last, basic question. They had no problem with the age, grade, or sex/gender questions—on these measures they did fine. But when it came to race, their responses became evasive and dissonant. Numerous students gave responses that were ironic instead of genuine. For example, one student abruptly took on a silly and fake British accent and said, "I'm the whiteness of the white boys." Bucholtz described this response as a mock-celebration of his "affiliation with whiteness." Other students feigned ignorance or became visibly uncomfortable. For example, after saying "white," they would add a qualifying statement like "I guess" or "I don't know." Bucholtz didn't encounter any significant evasion or discomfort among students of color in response to the same question.

It's clear through the rest of each individual interview that the students giving Bucholtz such disjointed responses do, in fact, know they're white. Their responses aren't about them actually being confused about their identity. Instead, they seem to be some kind of demonstration of their awareness about how problematic it is to embody an identity marked "white" in a white racial hierarchy. Given the racial diversity and multiculturalism commitments of the school, students' awareness of hierarchy and their own whiteness would have been particularly acute. It makes sense that it was when the specter of being associated with whiteness was explicitly raised, even through a question as seemingly innocent as "what's your race/ethnicity," that such strange reactions were the result.

What Bucholtz ultimately concludes is going on with these teenagers is relevant to the distress that seems to be going on in P.'s question to her mom. Throughout her study, Bucholtz finds among white students a largely subconscious, but very real and pervasive fear. Students are afraid that if they admit they are white *without*, in the same moment, demonstrating some reluctance about being white or without distancing themselves from white identity (that is, by mocking whiteness, or vaguely evading the question), they might be seen as endorsing racism. In other words, white identity and white dominance are so tangled up together that asking about one automatically raised the other. So they get silly, snarky, or tongue-tied when put in a position to have to say, "I'm white."

If we recognize how entangled hierarchy and identity are, these strange responses make a lot of sense. These students are attempting to create a kind of gap between themselves and racism. They're trying to generate distance between who they are as people who are white and the widespread cultural recognition that racism is a white thing. It would seem they're experiencing a context in which those two things are deeply conflated. Even if much of their experience registers mostly at the subconscious level, this conflation and context causes them discomfort.

Bucholtz discovers something else that seems to vex these white high school students as well. She finds that whiteness in this school is associated with "cultural blandness and lack of coolness."[2] Sometimes this comes up as a kind of joke. But sometimes it's clear this is a highly painful experience for these youth. And it's here this study gets particularly useful in terms of more fully understanding the reason diversity can be so confusing for white kids.

A palpable perception of "white uncoolness" is partially related to the fear among white students that being white means one is (or is going to be perceived as) innately racist. Imagine being immersed in a context where celebrating racial diversity is the publicly endorsed norm. You know very well, though, that celebrating your own specific diversity—whiteness—is forbidden. The reality that this is forbidden is probably not openly acknowledged or explored, however.

How could whiteness be or become anything other than uncool in such a context? You can't embrace your race while everyone else gets to do so. You can't participate positively and make a contribution to racial diversity. Meanwhile, you're supposed to simultaneously love engaging your (much cooler) peers across lines of difference. It seems to me all the students in this high school have been set up for failure.

Distress about the possibility that being white makes one innately racist, unaddressed feelings that one is inescapably "uncool" (which is hard for most people, but especially for teenagers), or some combination of both are uniquely related to the experience of being white in a society in which white identity puts one on the side of "unjust benefit" or "privilege" in regard to racism. The distress this experience brings often leads to resentment among white kids. Add the presence of collective racial tensions emerging out of larger racial scripts to this distress, and it's not hard to see how we can end up with full-blown racial tinderboxes all over the place in this society, even in high schools committed to multicultural education.

In fact, Bucholtz does find white resentment among the students she interviews. She finds that students at this diverse high school intentionally committed to teaching diversity are every bit as racially self-segregated as are students in schools where diversity is present but not given explicit attention. A focus on multiculturalism didn't change students' interracial relationships one iota. Bucholtz also finds that many of the white students she interviews are cynical about, completely disinterested in, and, in some cases, even downright hostile to the school's focus on diversity. Notably, this dynamic has nothing do with conservative politics. This school is located in a politically liberal part of northern California.

All of these findings are precisely the opposite outcomes hoped for by way of the school's multicultural focus, of course. And it's worth focusing on this phenomenon for precisely that reason. Bucholtz's discovery points to a different challenge related to diversity than the one we explored in relationship to preexisting racial scripts causing diversity alone to fail as a strategy. The challenge here has to do with white kids' experience of diversity relative to their own specific identity. The extent to which white is a vexed location makes it difficult for whites to authentically embrace diversity, let alone embrace it deeply.

I've been convinced for a long time that one major reason behind our failures around diversity, even in educational or other contexts (faith communities, for example) where it is genuinely valued, has do with the fact that diversity provides no meaningful way for white people to plug in. White people's individual racism is often blamed for ongoing failure to realize diversity. Certainly this is a major factor. But the specific obstacles caused by whiteness run much deeper and are more complex than explicit racism. They have to do with the meaning of white identity in an unjust society, and with what that vexed location does even to folks who genuinely want to embrace difference.

Bucholtz's findings seem to support my sense of things here. She determines that white students' negative views toward diversity are a symptom of not having access to what she calls a "meaningful 'ethnoracial' identity."[3] In other words, white students don't have an embraceable, positive, meaningful racial identity in a context where everyone else gets to have one. As a result they become deeply alienated from the whole enterprise of diversity—and, I would add, by extension they become alienated from commitments to racial justice.

In many ways the problem that P.'s story and Bucholtz's study bring into focus has to do with the issue *Raising White Kids* is devoted to unpacking. Meaningful, embraceable white identity is a problem because of the reality of a pervasive presence of white supremacy in this society. This social position creates unique conundrums for white people—including children and youth—seeking to work for racial justice. There's no simple fix here. Until white supremacy is eradicated, white identity will continue to be a complex experience—an identity that just can't, in and of itself, be embraced. White is just not a parallel identity to Black, Latino/a, Cherokee, Chinese American, Mexican American or any other social/racial/ethnic identity. It's an identity that requires white people who seek to grow our antiracism and our justice commitments a unique type of journey. And this is a journey for which we have few models.

But just because there's no simple fix doesn't mean we can leave this real problem unaddressed. In fact, we can't ignore it if we're serious about raising white children who are empowered in regard to antiracism, comfortable in their own skin, and able to function well in diverse racial contexts. Being white is a painful and vexed location in the context of awareness of justice. We have to take this seriously and practice talking about it.

Race-conscious parenting means creating opportunities for our children to reflect on the emotionally difficult truth of whiteness. Older children have experienced such difficult truths long before they have words for them. But for lots of understandable reasons, this emotionally difficult truth unique to white people is rarely discussed in environments where diversity is being valued. So our children learn silence around this experience very quickly. If race is taboo in so many ways, it is even more taboo to talk openly about what it's like to be white. Finding ways to support white children and youth (such as those in the Bucholtz study) in so doing is, thus, urgent.

Learning to See (and to Create) a "Gap"

As parents we need to cultivate constructive strategies to directly respond to this challenge of meaningful racial identity. In the big-picture response to P., it is critical, for example, that P.'s mom finds a way to support P. in starting to disentangle her selfhood from the negative and defeating sense that being white means being unequivocally racist.

This is long-term developmental work of precisely the sort explored in our discussion of white racial identity development theory (in chapter 3). P. isn't too young to begin this work: the moment children begin to articulate distress about being white relative to their recognition of racism, however confused that recognition may be, it's time to begin.

Indeed, distress about being white can emerge at ages younger than age ten or can show up much later. When white children and youth are offered honest assessments of race and truthful histories about or analysis of contemporary racial realities in the United States, it's almost inevitable we parents and teachers will find ourselves engaging painful questions about white people at some points.

> Dialogue about white complicity will at some point become the center of the discussion. This is good. It's important. But it's also very hard.

I recall a conversation with my daughter when she was about six after a period of time in which we had been talking a lot about Native peoples and the mountain home we now live in during the summers. The specific dialogues have long since become blurry to me, but over a period of weeks I had repeatedly invoked the Ute people, whose place this was before colonization. I told her that their dispossession was directly linked to this place now being a place where mostly white people live.

Through the course of these conversations we ended up in larger discussions of the triangle of unjust relationships among indigenous, African, and European peoples that forged the United States. This dialogue proceeded in a back-and-forth fashion. I would share things as we just moved through our day-to-day lives in this location, and she would usually respond in a pretty typical six-year-old way—with question after question after question, replete with lots of whys and hows.

I recall that at some point in these conversations, my daughter asked me (and I believe she did so more than once), "Did all the Europeans do such bad things?" At another point, she explicitly asked, "Are we white?" and "Does that mean we come from Europeans?"

These questions felt painful to me. But of course, I said *yes*, in the big picture Europeans simply didn't belong on this land at all because it wasn't theirs and that, *yes*, Europeans as a group were the ones who engaged in or supported the enslavement of African peoples. And I said that *yes*, our family was, indeed, descended from Europeans. In fact, I told her, specific members of my own family participated in these specific injustices in very explicit ways.

223

But I also told her there were a few white people who knew that what was being done was wrong and who tried to find ways to resist. I told her, for example, I knew of at least one person in our family who had held African peoples as slaves, but that we also had at least one person who had fought to end slavery even before most other white people did that. I remember John Brown coming up in this conversation.

I also told my daughter that my connection, as a white person, to this history is one of the reasons I work so hard to learn about injustice and to constantly work *for* justice. Most important, I told her we can always make different choices than our ancestors did—that it's our job to actively make different choices and work for justice and fairness today, especially if we're white.

This was a younger-than-high-school recognition of how vexed is the position of being white. But I regularly see older-than-high-school versions of this recognition too. So many feelings and frustrations emerge in my college classrooms when I engage students in a truer version of racial history than most have ever engaged before, or in frank assessments of the racial climate at our university. Last year, I taught Dakota scholar and activist Waziyatawin's incredible book *What Does Justice Look Like?* in one of my classes. Waziyatawin's detailed history of how Minnesota became a state elicited reactions from all students that ran the gamut from horror at the history itself to outrage at having never been taught the history. White students were devastated in a particular way and none more so than the several who were from Minnesota. They all felt complicit. They all struggled with

224

how they would now "go home." White had come to seem to them synonymous with violence of unimaginable proportions and defined today in Minnesota by the ongoing legacies of these histories in contemporary social, economic, and land relations. Their embodiment as white people became deeply, literally, physically uncomfortable. This induced a college-age version of what was going on for my daughter when she asked me if we descended from Europeans.

The point of these examples is to emphasize that when we're engaged in a sustained practice of having honest conversations about race with our children, at whatever the age it happens, it will happen: dialogue about white complicity will at some point become the center of the discussion. This is good. It's important. But it's also very hard.

Setting aside that her mom couldn't quite understand exactly what had happened, in the case of P.—whose pain is real—support doesn't mean rushing in to assure her she's not racist. It doesn't mean downplaying or avoiding discussion of the reality that, given the nature of our society, yes, white people are all complicit with racism. Yes, we are complicit with almost unavoidable ease. So, in a sense, "Yes P., you (like me) are racist."

Whatever else may be going on, P. is showing something of an awareness of the real moral crisis that those of us who are white and who want to be healthy (that is, antiracist) live with every day. As a white person, this is something P. must contend with. Her plea here is a sign she is engaged in critical developmental work.

But in the bigger picture, support does mean dialogue and

work aimed at inviting P. to see the gap between herself, even as a white person, and *racist systems*. It means finding ways to invite her to strategize how she can actually make that gap even larger through active, antiracist behaviors.

The gap I'm describing here is the same one Bucholtz's white students unsuccessfully tried to create by rhetorically evading Bucholtz's question about racial identity. As parents, we need to support children in creating distance between "being white" and "racist" in larger contexts in which these are conflated. But creating such distance is not about allowing them to downplay their complicity with racism or evade their whiteness. It's not about saying, "P., you may be white, but you are a good person." We have to be direct and authentic with them about how complicit we are and how much we are all impacted by the racism we breathe in and benefit from as white people.

Let's Talk Strategies

Creating distance is about finding strategies that interrupt kids when they conflate "white" and "racist" in ways that can be so self-defeating they're likely to cause developmental regression—and potentially more active racism. I'm taking a lesson from Bucholtz's findings here. White students in Bucholtz's study were hostile to the whole emphasis on diversity in large part because the pain of "no gap" (combined with being "uncool") was just too great. If we want a different result in terms of our children's relationships to diversity—and by extension antiracism and justice—we have to work for it.

One strategy emerges from understanding the precise reasons diversity is so confusing. For example, when we talk about something like Black history and culture, a significant dimension of what we are talking about is the resistance, creativity, and agency African American people have lived in response to the domination of white racial hierarchy. Learning about the histories and cultures of communities of color is critical for white children and youth.

But parents must also offer white children and youth a meaningful place to stand or a way to meaningfully participate in diversity. This isn't a suggestion to say to our kids, let's celebrate white culture. Rather, offering white youth a meaningful place to stand means sharing with them models of white people—those who have lived in the past and those who are alive and active today—who live agency against racism. Such a commitment doesn't mean shifting focus away from people of color or downplaying the painful history of white complicity with racism. It means recognizing that white children desperately need examples of people who have created a gap between who they were and are as selves and the systems of white supremacy in which they lived and live.

So, for example, in terms of offering meaningful participation in the context of diversity, this doesn't mean celebrating George Washington because he founded the nation and was white! It means making sure we lift up and celebrate someone like John Brown, who was white and was so horrified by slavery he acted to end it.

It doesn't mean overstating to our kids how much better things became as a result of the civil rights movement or how

227

many white people were involved in it. (Let's not forget that many white people still alive today opposed or were apathetic toward the civil rights movement at the time.) It does mean sharing with them stories about people like Joan Trumpauer Mulholland. She was a young white woman from Virginia so active in protesting segregation as part of Black-led organizing (notably during the freedom rides in 1961) that she was arrested. You can still find her mug shot online. Her family disowned her.[4]

It doesn't mean that when we teach our children about the reality of police violence against African American communities we make sure to tell them that most white police officers are good. It means sharing images with them of white people who are so horrified by police violence against Black people that they show up to protest with, and in support of, Black communities as they challenge this violence.

I can't say enough that the teaching here is not that there is a strong justice-commitment in white culture. There isn't. This would be a false teaching. And, frankly, there is no abstract or easy answer to the diversity problem for white kids. In fact, a core hope behind this book is that by differently raising white kids today, we contribute to creating a future in which this real problem of white identity is less difficult because models of antiracist white commitment become so much more increased (and white supremacy's power decreased).

The point is that we need to practice taking the same postures we discussed before—those that make us fellow pilgrims with our children. Then we need to find routes to invite them to see and create concrete ways, places, and activities through which we disallow "being white" from determining our behavior or allegiances. We need to help them experience in their own bodies that being white doesn't have to only or primarily mean complicity with racist structures.

This line of thinking, too, goes deeper than teaching them antiracist behaviors or offering them antiracist models. It is those things. But it is also being explicit about whiteness as we do so:

"Look, this person is white."

"Look, that person was white."

"Look, this person knew racism was wrong and challenged it very courageously."

"How did it feel to you as a white kid to hear that thing that was said?"

"Did that situation make you feel bad about being white?"

"What actions could we take as white people in that situation; would our action change how it feels to be white?"

Calling attention to the presence of whiteness matters in antiracist-focused situations and dialogues. It matters not to falsely affirm white people for justice work. Rather, doing so generates necessary reflection on the experience of and more embodied self-awareness of being white.

The strategies we each use are going to be context specific, enough so that it's difficult to offer these in a book such as this. But in terms of broad principles, these strategies have to do with engaging our children to better understand their experience of their own identity in their immediate social contexts and supporting them in taking action in those contexts. Action is a critical anecdote to the kind of white despair that emerges from having your identity conflated with "oppressor," despair that not only harms white children but which turns into resentment of diversity or people of color, and sometimes into appropriation of people of color's cultures when white youth try to fill the uncool void.

There's no simple or blanket way to enable white children to cultivate meaningful "ethnoracial identity." Social identities only become meaningful through collective and sustained actions over time in public and political ways. One white person cannot on her own change the collective meaning of her white identity by antiracist action.

But one person can continually change her own relationship with her white identity. We can enable our children to cultivate a meaningful sense of their identity as people who live for justice and in resistance to racism *despite* being from a people from whom such behaviors are rarely expected (and, unfortunately, too rarely come).

When we make it a priority to support our children in taking action against racism or participating with them in such action, we're not just building their antiracist skill set. This is also developmental work in terms of their sense of selfhood. We want girls to feel strong. We want children of color to feel smart. We want gender-nonconforming children to feel bold.

So we teach all of these diverse kids specific ways to cultivate a sense of themselves that runs counter to the meanings that systems of sexism, racism, and heterosexism impose on their social identity. We need to so something parallel for white kids, only in reverse. Just as we need to support boys in growing feminist-committed and antisexist ways of experiencing their own gender, and gender-conforming children in embracing more gender-fluid ways to experience their own identity and embrace the identities of others, we need to support white kids in cultivating ways to experience antiracism as a way to make more sense out of, and gain a foothold in, their relationship to their own white racial identity.

Taking action enables our children to move through the guilt-, resentment-, and anxiety-laden stages of white racial identity development. Living and experiencing agency mitigates the experience of being white as being sentenced to a permanent state of uncoolness at best, and racism at worst. Doing so gives our kids one route into meaningful participation in diversity frameworks. (As an added bonus, their action-agency makes them more likely to be able to create authentic and sustainable interracial relationships.)

This bigger picture engagement with P., then, means seeking out clearer parental understanding of what the racial climate and challenges are at P.'s school. Seeing what types of student relationships exist there, what kind of racial dynamics exist in the classrooms, and finding ways to ask P. about this and support her in imagining herself as someone who can make a justice-committed impact, are all part of what's needed in this moment. The specifics will depend on the school. So let me brainstorm some ways this could have looked in my own middle-school context in order to offer some hypothetical examples.

For example, there were all kinds of student-initiated clubs and after-school activities at my school, where powerful relationship building happened through student investment in shared projects. What might it look like to support our kids in creating some kind of racial justice club? A middle-school model might look like a racial-justice version of the Gay Straight Alliance (GSA), which has become something of a fixture on the middle school and high school scene. Finding buy-in and identifying a racially diverse set of students to initiate such a venture would be a must. Capable adult guidance in such a venture would be important too. But longer-term commitment to such a project, if done well, could have a powerful impact on the racial climate at a school. This would be so much more effective than the one-shot racial dialogue panels schools often host after some sort of racialized incident happens, or the one-dimensional value of "embrace difference" that happens at many schools.

Here's another example. In my middle school, racial tracking had begun to take hold. Tracking was intense by high school. Another route to engaging children and youth would be significant parental engagement to challenge this injustice at the local level. What might have happened in my life, the lives of students of color, and the overall racial climate at my school, for example, if my parents and the parents of other white students had worked across racial lines to raise questions about which students were being put in which classes, which programs were receiving what resources? What might have happened if they engaged the school to insist on equity?

In fact, very likely parents of color were already asking such questions and engaged in such work. More often than not, wherever people of color are present (living, working, going to school) some kind of justice organizing is already being done. Before starting something ourselves, white parents should look up and see where people of color–led efforts along these lines are already happening. So here again, finding the appropriate collaborators and stakeholders would be important groundwork, before finding ways to engage the teachers and administration directly, and then involving students in the process.

Perhaps it's not so much about what P. does at school. When I was in middle school, my peers and teachers knew all about my deep commitment to soccer and my family's highly devoted religious life. I brought these to school in any number of ways: talked about them, wrote reports on them when I got to choose a topic, and so on. A different type of support in creating a gap, and enabling white students to more ably engage diversity, is by involving them in deeply committed justice-work outside of school. The more such work is part of how our kids move through the world, the more it shows up in how they engage at school. Antiracist practices become part of how our youth understand themselves.

Perhaps in P.'s case, altogether different routes in would be necessary. But whatever these might be, we need to understand that improvements in white children's relationships to diversity aren't going to just come with time. Active interventions are required to create ways for white youth to experience antiracist agency. But with an experience of such agency a different relationship to their white identity can emerge. And a different relationship to their own racial identity is necessary for them to be able to engage diversity ably.

I'm brainstorming all of the above suggestions from a distance. But here's the major takeaway. Our children are not and should not perceive themselves to be generic Americans. Nor should they only reluctantly confess, "I'm white, I guess." They need to not be left to internalize the fears expressed in "Mom, am I racist?" What they need is to be eventually able to say, "I'm white, and I'm also an antiracist-committed person active in taking a stand against racism and injustice when I see it."

Conceptual Clarity

At this point I want to return to the confusion that's more on the surface of P.'s exchange with her mom. As much as I suspect that emerging feelings about being white are underneath P.'s distress, the confusion she explicitly names also has to do with a conceptual understanding of racism.

When a girl made a disparaging comment to my nephew, my sister told T. the girl was being racist because she was trying to make him feel bad about his skin color. When I talk about larger racial histories of system inequity or even racial violence with my children, who are six and eight, I know what they mostly hear—even what they sometimes say back to me—gets simplified into "that person, or those people, must not like Black people or Latino/a people."

Before a certain point of intellectual development, young children are likely to hold on to such simplistic and individualistic notions of what constitutes racism. Nonetheless, Debra Van Ausdale and Joe Feagin remind us how important it is to teach children early about racist structures anyway.

> Talk about the fact that the social world we live in is often unfair to people of color simply because they are people of color and that persisting racial-ethnic inequalities are unjust and morally wrong. Make it clear that racial-ethnic prejudice and discrimination are part of a larger society that needs reform and not just something that individuals do.[5]

Without such a larger framework, our children will observe racial disparities for themselves and explain them by presuming something must be wrong with people of color. In contrast, when we do introduce these larger frameworks early in life, our kids learn to understand the structures we live in. They become poised for conceptual clarity to kick in, much earlier than we might expect.

If offered in age-appropriate ways, a ten-year-old like P. is certainly ready to begin to develop such clarity. And supporting children to untangle different dimensions of racism is vital for building their language and analytical understanding.

Understanding will support confidence in racially difficult encounters at school or in other social settings.

One of Beverly Daniel Tatum's analogies, which speaks to different dimensions of racism, would be brilliantly accessible to a ten-year-old, for example. This is a useful conversation tool. Tatum describes racism as a moving walkway (like the kind at airports). All white people are riding the walkway whether we want to or not. We didn't choose to be placed on the walkway. But we do have choices we can make about what we do while we are riding it.

Anytime we stand still on the moving walkway and let it take us where it's already going, we are participating in racism. Tatum calls this "passive racism." It's the kind of racism that happens if you just do nothing. "Active racism" is when people choose to walk in the same direction the walkway's already going. Either standing still or walking with it are individual choices white people make about how to act and relate to the moving walkway.[6]

This part of Tatum's analogy can help us talk with children about the relationship of white people to racism. Whatever type of participation we engage in—for example, actively believing negative stereotypes about people of color, being silent when we hear others endorse stereotypes, or acting on our own biases against people of color—this part of the analogy is a great way to invite children to understand individual racism and our relationship to it.

I like to take Tatum's analogy a step further to support younger children in developing an understanding of structural racism. Structural racism is the thing that built the walkway, put us all on it, and set it running in a particular direction in the first place: the plans that were drawn up, the money it took, the workers who were paid to build it and keep getting paid to maintain it. Structural racism is the larger system behind the walkway's existence; the things that keep it going—which sometimes we don't even see.

Using an analogy like this has many short- and long-term gains. First, it's a great way to build accessible scaffolding with our kids to which we start to help them add increasing conceptual understanding about different dimensions of racism. It offers a way to talk about how dimensions of racism, though distinct, interact with one another. This analogy, then, can help us parse out with them and make sense of things that are happening in the world (or can help us do so when they come to us later for help understanding). This kind of analogy enables our kids to begin to recognize, and eventually describe and articulate for themselves, various dimensions of racism as they encounter them in the world.

> When justice is the deepest goal and value, developing an understanding of equity, in contrast to equality, is key.

Second, this analogy offers an accessible way to get at white people's own individual and collective relationship with various forms of racism. Let's talk about the moving walkway and where we are standing on it. Let's see what it is about the experiences we're having that pertain to the moving walkway, the system that built it, and possibilities for our individual reaction to the walkway in a given moment.

The walkway analogy supports intellectual clarity. This can enable children to be more resilient and equipped when they encounter race and racism talk in their lives. Much more important, it's also an image that lends itself wonderfully to looking into our daily lives, contexts, and social experiences with our kids and setting some concrete goals. The goal is to always walk, run, and develop more stamina to keep running in precisely the opposite direction from the one the moving walkway is taking us. In any given moment, situation, or context, then, we can ask and explore with our kids, "Where is the walkway taking us right now? What could we to do to run against it?"

An analogy like this enables our children to be ready to engage in dialogues about and analysis of racism. But it also becomes a ritualized discussion that sets the stage for the ongoing life practices of creating larger and larger gaps. It helps our white children understand that *we are not the moving walkway* itself. And we didn't build the walkway. But we are on the walkway whether we want to be or not. Antiracism necessarily requires us to make choices everyday to do something about how we situate ourselves on the walkway. This analogy can help our kids envision and, through taking meaningful action, distinguish themselves as people from the system of racism—without downplaying how complicit their whiteness makes them.

A different concept that can offer our children routes out of the self-defeating conflation of *white* with *racist* might be useful in the type of situation presented by P.'s distressed, "Mom, am I racist?" That is the concept of white privilege. It could be that a conversation about privilege and the ways white people experience privilege—even when we don't ask for it—would help P.'s distress.

Introducing the concept of white privilege might help to de-escalate the deeply fraught and powerful content *racist* has already come to have for her. It might be useful to temporarily direct her away from the *r* word and make clear that white privilege is not something she is guilty of—it's something white people inherit. Like the moving walkway analogy, however, introducing this notion needs to be done while keeping on the table the choices we all make about how complicit we will remain with white privilege. And, eventually, connecting the decision to passively accept white privilege to active racism, which supports the systems of racial injustice, must come back into the dialogue.

There are so many useful images and tools, appropriate and accessible for different age groups, for introducing racism and its various dimensions to children. Here's one more I find to be especially useful for children and youth. Teaching our children the distinction between the value of *equality* and *equity* is important because our kids receive a lot of messages from the broader culture about equality being the most important thing when it comes to race.

To this end, there's an outstanding drawing (the first version I encountered was created by the Interaction Institute for Social Change) that shows three people of very different heights standing next to one another. Their backs are toward us. They're all peering over the fence trying to see a baseball game.[7]

In the image that illustrates what it looks like to value equality, each of the three people has been handed a box to stand on to help them see over the fence. The boxes are all of equal size.

> As with everything else related to raising white kids for racial justice, our own persistence matters.

As a result, the tallest person is now able to see the game beautifully. The eyes of the person of medium height are now at about fence level. He can see the game but he's still straining to do so. The shortest of the three people still can't see the game at all. He was treated equally—his box was the same size as the other two people. But equality doesn't ask about how things turn out, which in this case isn't very well.

In the image that illustrates equity, each of the three people is also given a box to stand on so they can see the game better. But in dramatic contrast to the first image, these boxes are of different heights. The shortest person is given the tallest box and the tallest person the shortest box. As a result, each person is able to see the game at the same level as the other two. Three different-sized boxes produce an equitable outcome. In fact, if you looked at the people from the baseball field side of things (in which case the boxes would be behind the fence and hidden from view) you would assume these three people were all exactly the same height. Unequally sized boxes created equity. When justice is the deepest goal and value, developing an understanding of equity, in contrast to equality, is key to our children's ability to be good interlocutors engaging race and racism in the world.

These are just a few examples of ways to more deeply develop children's conceptual clarity. There are other tools that make such concepts accessible that we can avail ourselves of. In fact, some of the most important gifts we can give ourselves as parents include at least the following.

- We can make regular use of the many excellent resources that already exist, created by similarly justice-committed educators and parents (a number of which are listed in "Other Resources").
- We can remember or learn that we aren't the first to struggle to figure out how to teach race and anti-racism to white kids and we don't have to reinvent the wheel.
- And I can't stress this enough: We can reach out to connect with communities of other parents who are also actively building their own capacity for race-conscious, racial-justice parenting.

This last idea may mean participating in online forums. It might be through intentionally cultivating these dialogues in our existing friendships with other parents who share a commitment to racial justice and who are, in their specific journeys with their specific and different kids, also looking for ways to do it well. It might even be engaging with other people who already gather to talk about these issues (such groups do exist; see "Other Resources") or creating such groups ourselves. The ability to connect, share strategies, brainstorm, and be encouraged and supported by other parents cannot be overestimated.

"Mom, Am I Racist?"

P.'s mom is one of my best friends. I know she made a valiant effort that day both to unpack what had happened at school and to support a productive, race-conscious dialogue with P. in that moment. Knowing her justice commitments and what a great communicator she is, I can imagine any number of productive exchanges that may have proceeded to take place that day.

So let's imagine what some of those routes into learning might have looked like in a conversation such as this. Because for many of us, an experience like my friend had with P. might find us, at first, a bit tongue-tied as to where to begin. Thinking through the following possibilities is a way to continue building our moral vision for how we, in our own relationships with our kids, take a posture of accompaniment, follow our children's lead, lay groundwork for ongoing dialogue, and share our values with them when such incredible opportunities present themselves.

- "So what do you think 'racist' is?"
- "What do you think your classmates were saying you had done? Namely, what do *they* think 'racist' is?"

- "You sound really upset about what happened. What are you feeling right now? What are you worried is going to happen?"
- "Why do you think your classmates thought you were being racist? Do you ever feel like racism happens in your class or at your school? Do you think your classmates are against racism? What does that mean?"
- "Were the kids who were calling you 'racist' white kids? Black kids? Latino/a kids? Why do you think white kids would say that? Were they making a joke out of racism? Why do you think Black or Latino/a kids would say that? Do they experience racism at school sometimes and so maybe thought that's what you were up to?"
- "You know, have you heard people say things like, 'race doesn't matter, we're all the same underneath our skin' or 'treat everyone the same, no matter what?' I wonder if, when you asked for a brown crayon, your friends thought you were being racist because you were drawing a picture where you decided to use brown for someone's skin color. That doesn't make you racist at all! I think they might have said that because they think 'race doesn't matter.' But we know race matters a lot, and we want to see and celebrate all different kinds of people."
- "What does your teacher say about racism at school? Does she/he ever talk about it?"

- "Do white kids and Latino/a kids and Black kids play together at your school? Do they ever call each other racist? Have you ever seen someone behave in a way that made you think *they* were racist?"
- "You know, P., I'm sorry your feelings got so hurt today. I can tell it felt bad to you to have kids in your class call you racist. This whole thing makes me realize we need to talk a little bit more often about what racism is. I want to talk more about it so we can, as a family, better understand racism. I want us to do that so we can practice being a family that works really hard to fight against racism when it happens. So how about we . . . [fill in the blank]."

Race, diversity, racism, and racial difference are all difficult in the United States. Children of color don't become immune from the impact of race and racism just because their parents engage in consistent and thoughtful efforts to teach and insulate them. No less is true for white children. The most consistent and thoughtful efforts will not prevent race from being challenging for white kids. As with everything else related to raising white kids for racial justice, our own persistence matters. Continuing to show up for and be with our kids as parents and caretakers or to courageously teach white kids as educators combined with daily self-reminders that we don't have to have all the answers but just need to continue to ask good questions and find good resources will go a long in cultivating their persistence as well.

Takeaways

✓ As kids become aware of the concepts of racism, diversity, white privilege, and so on, they can become confused or anxious. Quips like "That's so racist!" have become common in youth culture. Parents must help develop clarity about the dimensions of racism.

✓ Being white is a painful and vexed location in the context of awareness of injustice—particularly for kids. This makes it difficult for whites to authentically embrace diversity, let alone embrace it deeply.

✓ Despite it being taboo, we need to support white children in scrutinizing and talking about how they feel about being white, what being white does or does not have to do with "being racist," and even about how confusing diversity can be for them, given their whiteness.

✓ This dialogue and work help white kids find ways to create a gap between themselves and racism: white doesn't have to only mean "racist"—namely, you can be white and engage in antiracist activity, without downplaying the racism we breathe in and benefit from as white people.

✓ Because of the system we live in, white people are all complicit with racism and we must help our kids contend with this even while we equip them with lots of explanations about concepts like inherited privilege, equity in contrast to equality, and the analogy of racism as a moving sidewalk!

CHAPTER 7

What Does Resistance Look Like?

If you had asked my soon-to-be six-year-old about immigration during the presidential election cycle of 2016, E. would have told you this: "Donald Trump doesn't want people to be able to feed their babies. He thinks that the law is more important than people being able to feed their babies. I think being able to feed your baby is more important than following the law."

There's so much uncharted territory in parenting. This is true when raising kids in a nation experiencing the best of times and in regard to any number of issues. But there's nothing easy about *these* times and race is uniquely difficult. Raising white kids differently than most of us were raised, with few road maps, at a time when the failures of decades of color-blind parenting and tepid attempts to celebrate difference have been exposed is difficult enough. But with news cycles bleeding with stories of Black people killed by police, Latino/a peoples being terrorized by Immigration and Customs Enforcement (ICE)—

whether they're immigrants or not—and rising numbers of hate crimes against Muslim and Jewish people, the words *difficult* and *uncharted territory* scarcely capture it.

Those of us raising children may feel like we're constantly watching and waiting and measuring. This may be especially true if we're raising white children we long to equip as participants in creating a more just and flourishing future for all. I know my partner and I often feel like we're second-guessing ourselves as we parent our two white kids in this terrain and in these times.

As increasingly hateful racial rhetoric became more widespread and pervasive in the public square leading up to and after the 2016 presidential election, we struggled with how to talk about it with our children. We worried about finding the line between communicating our values and engaging them in moral deliberations, while not using them as props in larger political debates in which they were only mimics of us.

I don't know that we got it right all the way. But I did end up feeling good about the perspective E. eventually took on the stakes in the political fight over immigration. I ended up in awe of her ability to listen to us and to break it down and see moral complexity in a way that made sense to her young mind and heart. This seemed particularly impressive to me since we spend a lot of time telling kids they're supposed to follow the rules.

But as awesome as I think my child is, I don't actually think she's particularly unique on this front. I think the more that more of us engage our children explicitly, the more often we do and will find ourselves similarly impressed.

I hold on tightly to the moments in which I find myself more awed by my kids' insights and wisdom than I am overcome by my own fears and missteps. I want nothing more than for those reading this book to experience and hold on to such moments as well. And it's my deepest hope that in the process of doing so, we collectively create communities of parent-peers. Such communities could generate and invigorate a society-wide dialogue about how parents of white children can step into the unknowns, chart what is mostly still uncharted, and become resilient participants alongside parents of children of color who are already at it and have long been so. It's my deepest longing that this book will enable more of us to deepen our active commitment to *everyone's children* by drawing more of us into the larger movement of social and racial justice. For, despite all that remains truly difficult and how far we have to go, such a movement is alive and resilient in this nation. And it needs all of us to be *all in*.

No book could ever speak to all that needs to be addressed nor offer a complete list of perfect responses for every challenging moment in our parental lives. No one book can address all of the larger, unanswered questions about how to effectively raise race-conscious, justice-committed white children in these days and times. At the end of the day, what resistance looks like still remains up to each of us to envision, create, and live out the best we can.

As we begin to bring the explorations we've moved through in these pages to an end, then, I want to reflect on several other dimensions of race-conscious parenting that deserve

focus. These dimensions augment and build on other principles and practices already presented in *Raising White Kids*.
But they also lift up deeper insights and more open questions
about some of the more difficult and rewarding emotional
aspects of cultivating antiracism and justice commitments in
our children.

White Children and Black Lives Matter

In September 2016, within a period of two weeks, Terence
Crutcher and Keith Lamont Scott, two Black men, were shot
and killed by police. Tulsa, Oklahoma, and Charlotte, North
Carolina, the cities where these men were killed, each erupted
in protest. During this period of time I had the following
engagements with my children.

*We were driving to school and a segment on National
Public Radio came on about the protests taking place
in Charlotte. I noticed my kids get quiet in the back
seat and made a conscious decision to let the story play.
When it was over, I turned the radio off before another
story could come on. Then I kept driving and said
nothing. After a few moments of quiet my seven-year-old
said, "Mama, if you were in Charlotte right now, I bet
you'd put on your Black Lives Matter T-shirt and go out
there with them."*

"I probably would, H," I said.

*Over the next few minutes we pursued a conversa-
tion about the story. My kids' respective understanding*

of what they had just heard varied, which made sense given their two-year age difference. But they both asked questions and I tried to answer them and follow their lead. I felt myself dancing the line between too much information and not enough. But I tried to be truthful and clear.

I explained that once again, in two different places in the country, police officers had killed Black people. I said that people all over the county, but especially African Americans, were very angry.

At some point in this conversation E. (who was five at the time) asked me, "Mama, some police officers are safe, aren't they?"

"Yes, E." I said, "Some police officers are safe. But some police keep killing Black people. People are protesting because they want that to stop. Nobody should have to be afraid of the police. Actually, even the police officers who are safe should be trying to make this stop."

"Is this kind of like what happened to T. at school, with the Doritos?" E. asked. "Yes," I said, "this is happening because of racism."

In her final question, E. was referencing her cousin's encounter with racism, which I wrote about in chapter 3. It's worth noticing that this police conversation took place three full months after that conversation (and I don't think we'd spoken of the Doritos incident since). Our kids hold on to the dialogues we have with them in ways we may not be aware of

> Given the days we live in, if our hearts aren't broken we've already lost a core part of our humanity.

at the time. They actively use such dialogues, then, to interpret subsequent experiences and make sense out of other situations.

E.'s ability to connect the Doritos incident, which was much more concrete and accessible to her young self than this larger, more removed dialogue about police violence, is a great example of what we call in the world of teaching "scaffolding." Kids build upon what they've already built, which itself is built upon what came before that. If any of us needed a better example to be convinced of how effective it can be when we choose to talk about race early, directly, and often, I don't know that we could find one.

At this point the conversation ended. Both kids moved on to other appropriate topics and meaningful-to-them chatter about the upcoming day at school.

About a week later, students where I teach—led by Courtnei Caldwell—organized a solidarity rally. Once again, I debated the ethically loaded question of whether or not to take my kids with me and decided to give them the option.

> *"Girls, my students are organizing a protest. Remember when we talked about the men who were killed by police? My students are standing together, protesting, making clear they want this to stop. I'm going, and I'll take you if you want to go."*

Both of them: "Yes, we want to go. Can we make signs?"

"Sure." I said, "What are your signs going to say?" In unison they responded, "Black lives matter."

So here's how this story ended. My kids participated with vigor at the protest. In contrast to the ways they were present two years prior at the protest in response to Michael Brown's killer being acquitted (which I wrote about in chapter 2), they chanted, were fully engaged, and both had a sense of what was going on and why. They spent nearly an hour physically present with Black and Latino/a people, other people of color, and a few white people, who stood together to say *no*. They observed young people being brave and loud about the value of their own lives and about their right to be free. And they experienced adults and these same young people responding to them directly: asking them about their signs, affirming them, hugging them for making their five- and seven-year-old voices heard. All of this was powerful in terms of their racial identity development and their experience of antiracist agency in the world.

But it was in the middle part of the story that I learned, yet again, from my kids' insights and wisdom. I relearned that trying to be brave in this uncharted territory matters so much and that it's worth all the self-doubt and second-guessing such bravery can provoke in me.

I had walked downstairs to where my kids were making their signs to tell them it was time to go. Upon entering

253

*the playroom where they were working and seeing my
seven-year-old's sign, I caught my breath. Her gorgeous,
colorful sign said this [the spellings here are hers]:*

*"Black Lives Mater. They mater the same as white.
Stop killing them."*

*Then, below all of this script she had written the
names of people in her life that she loves. Her sign listed
them out this way:*

*"People that are Blak are: t. [her cousin] a.[her
cousin] tobi [her aunt]."*

I didn't only feel my breath catch when I took in this scene,
I felt my heart break as well. And almost every time I write
about or tell this story, I find myself weeping.

What I relearned and re-remembered from that gorgeous
but devastating sign and from witnessing firsthand my daughter's ability to connect the dots for herself was that these are
not times in which any of us can dare live without a broken
heart. Given the days we live in, if our hearts aren't broken
we've already lost a core part of our humanity.

One of the things I hold on to from that moment is a recognition that is devastating and beautiful all at the same time.
It's this: at this point in her life (nearly a year later as I write),
my daughter is a whole, wonderful, smart, kind, beautiful, and
very happy child. But she is also, in her eight-year-old and not-
quite-old-enough-to-fully-get-it way, herself living with a bit of
a broken heart.

The pain H. named during this experience had nothing to

do with me having ever told her explicitly: "Your aunt and cousins are Black. And police violence against Black people puts their lives in danger." I had never yet made the connection explicit for her. In retrospect, I wouldn't still. My parental sense, at least with my kids and at that age, is that doing so would be too intense as a direct teaching.

H. probably wouldn't even notice or name it as a kind of heartbreak. But by September 2016, my seven-year-old had hit an age at which she had put this all together for herself. She knew who the beloved people were in her life. Race-conscious parenting meant she understood that among these people, A., T., and Tobi were Black. She also knew that racism is a real thing with real consequences for people of color. And she had, thus, come to understand for herself exactly what the stakes were in going to this protest. On top of that she was still in touch with her own humanity, so in touch, in fact, that she would name the heartbreak of that recognition aloud.

(I was unsure and nervous about allowing H. to take a sign with her cousins' names on it—they were/are young children as well. Before allowing her to do so, I asked my sister and sister-in-law about it. My sister-in-law Tobi, whose name was also on the sign, called me back, asked for H., and told H. she loved her sign and thanked her for being an ally.)

There's so much to say about this experience, but at least three things are specifically worth lifting up in terms of parenting white children. Each of these pertain to the uncharted territory part of raising white kids.

First, the most truthful questions about raising white kids

aren't so much about how we best watch, wait, measure, and second-guess our attempts to teach them about justice and how we work for liberation and freedom. The real questions aren't practical how-to ones. They're not about doing it exactly right. The real and most truthful questions, I think, are what our children are going to teach us if we allow ourselves to be vulnerable enough to make it possible for them to do so. And what might they teach us if we then slow down and listen to them when they try?

The second thing also has to do with vulnerability—about allowing our kids to be vulnerable. We are going to constantly face the desire and tendency to insulate and protect our kids from heartbreak and fear. And we live in parenting cultures these days that place a high premium on protecting kids from all kinds of things—avoiding difficult feelings, making things easy for them, doing more for them than perhaps we should, trying to give them the best kind of experiences possible. The hopes embedded in a commitment to race-conscious parenting necessarily mean we bump up against such tendencies because such parenting requires us to expose our kids to hard realities. That can be tough.

Meanwhile, the reality of racial injustice raises genuinely difficult questions about what and how much to say: when to leave the radio on and when to turn it off. As one parent put it to me, "I don't want to lie to my kids about US history and our society. But how do I talk about histories of violence—for example, what slavery or treatment of Native Americans was like? I don't even let my eight-year-old watch violent television shows."

How much and in what detail are, in many ways, personal parental questions that have to do with many things, including the temperament of our particular children. At the same time, just as I felt myself viscerally react to the mom who said to me "I'm just glad she doesn't have to worry about any of it," I felt in the painful experience with my daughter the visceral knowledge that having chosen to allow her some heartbreak was, in fact, life-giving, humanizing, and necessary.

It's deeply necessary we let our children's hearts get broken a bit if they are going to remain able to recognize the humanity of their fellow humans whose lives are at stake in the system we live in. It's necessary if they are going to grow any rooted sense of themselves as part of a larger, multiracial community of people to whom they are committed, and with and for whom they must speak out and act.

What I'm describing here goes well beyond tactical questions about teaching kids how to engage in activism. It goes beyond saying, "Well, if Black kids have to learn about police violence then so should white kids—otherwise we are just embracing white privilege." This is certainly true, of course. But it's a rather surface assessment of the stakes.

What I'm getting at is creating space for our kids to move into their own deeply embodied relationships with injustice, as risky as that may feel. We need to create space for them to literally feel injustice and feel, touch, and ache from its real costs.

What I relearned in this painful experience with my daughters was that the entire enterprise of raising white kids for

257

racial justice requires a difficult, vulnerable recognition: in a world where human beings are suffering from human-caused injustice and violence, the humanity of even the youngest of our children is directly tied to their ability to identify with that suffering. And our children also need to explicitly come to understand that same truth.

It's understandable we want to protect our kids. But if we confuse finding age-appropriate ways to tell the truth about racial harm with overly insulating them, if we are too cautious because we are afraid it's just too much, if we withhold or sugarcoat truth because we don't want to cause them suffering, we withhold the very things they need to participate in deeper and more truthful ways of living. Indeed, we withhold the very things they most need to retain their humanity.

Complicating History (and the Stories People Tell) at Every Turn

The tendency to avoid leaving kids vulnerable by teaching them the truth about race isn't just manifested by parents. Another important relearning for me with my daughter came from an attempt by those responsible for her formal education to protect her and other kids in her first-grade class from painful truth.

We've already named the importance of teaching the histories of Native American, African American, Latino/a, and Asian American people. We've also talked about the significance of lifting up historical examples of white people who have engaged in antiracist action. But there's another aspect of history we need to pay attention to. This aspect is subtle but pervasive. It, too, deeply forms our children's consciousness. That is, we need to complicate the one-dimensional histories that even the most progressive schools tend to offer our children about white people.

One spring H. was running around endlessly singing the praises of George Washington. I was happy to see her so engaged with what she'd learned at school. But I was dismayed her public school (a school that I love and is spectacular in so many ways) had left her with such a one-dimensional view of history.

I struggled with how best to respond. Then one morning, she overheard the news on our kitchen radio about a politician charged with an ethics violation. (It's worth noticing that having good media on around the house can be a great strategy for opening up dialogue with our kids that otherwise might not unfold!)

"What's that about, Mama?" she asked.

I told her someone in the government had done something wrong, and she asked me how "an adult" who was "a leader" could possibly do something bad.

"Unfortunately," I responded, "a lot of our country's leaders have done bad things."

When her eyes grew big and she said, "Like who and what did they do?" I knew I had my answer.

"Well," I said, "you know how you've been running around here celebrating George Washington? We

259

always talk about George Washington fighting for freedom. But George Washington also owned Black people as slaves."

"He did?" H. was shocked and horrified.

"Yes." I said. "He really was only fighting for freedom for white people."

The best part of this dialogue came next.

"But, if he held slaves," H. asked, "why do we celebrate him as if he was such a great man?"

"You know what," I said, "that's a really great question. I'm not sure why we do. Why do you think we do that?"

From there H. and I mused together about her why question. I shared my ideas. I explained that it seems like it's hard for white Americans to admit that our ancestors did really bad things, maybe because it makes us feel bad. But I also told her that when we don't tell the whole truth we're also not talking honestly about Black people's history and Native American people's histories. We also act as if we don't care how they must have felt about someone like George Washington back then and that we don't care now about the ways they must feel about him today.

We also talked about the fact that we don't have to only feel bad about what our white ancestors did. We can find ways to challenge injustice and fix some of the things that they caused that are still impacting all of our lives today.

This dialogue worked directly against the compartmentalization we often use when teaching racial injustice in the United States. So much discussion, especially as it shows up in history books and at school, emphasizes (in ways more or less adequate) injustice as having happened to people of color and as having hurt them. It is much less common that the specific things specific white people actually did—including white people we celebrate as a nation—are part of the story.

We teach enslavement. We teach George Washington. But we never connect the two. This is very dangerous to our children's sense of history and to their consciousness overall.

A few years ago, I heard Melanie Morrison, a committed white antiracist educator, writer, and activist speak to a group of Christians about the powerful long-term effects of being socialized as white people.[1] Among what she attempted to get the gathered community to reflect on was the way white supremacy and white privilege, over time, impact the deepest parts of us. We have inherited intergenerational legacies of silence, of looking away, of pretending not to notice and of numbness to the pain of our racial legacies. The long-term effects of repressing the truth means we are people, she said, "who don't even know how to begin to feel what we feel." These legacies misshape our morality and our spirituality. And, she said, these affective and embodied layers of white supremacy's effects, therefore, make the journey into bold, antiracist embodiment arduous, soul-stretching work for white people.

I would add to Morrison's evocative words that all of this

261

also impacts our consciousness and our consciences. There are many teachings and social practices that contribute to ways whiteness accomplishes this harm. One of them is compartmentalized and fabricated celebrations of history and important historical figures.

Emphasizing the agency of people of color and the richness, value, complexity, and diversities of their lives outside and separate from an emphasis on racism and racial justice are important for antiracist consciousness. In a similar vein, it's important we teach about the ways antiracist-committed white people have shown up historically as well. But constantly complicating white racial history by also directly teaching our children about white people's complicity with racism is of the utmost importance to developing antiracist consciousness.

The point of my exchange with my daughter was not to uncritically condemn Washington or be anachronistic. And, of course, the argument that has most often come back at me when I've shared this dialogue I had with her in other places is that "George Washington was just doing what others at the time did" and it's not fair to judge him by today's standards.

But there are several problems with that argument. It erases the truth that Black people of the time knew slavery was wrong and that some white people knew it was wrong (even though they all lived in the same time period as did Washington). It ignores the truth that some white people who participated in the practice of slavery knew it was wrong and chose to do it anyway. It also suppresses the recognition that we live right now with all kinds of systems and practices that are today *just what everyone is doing.* The whole point is that it's too easy to be just like George Washington was then—too easy to just go along because it's how things are.

Our children need to wrestle with complex stories of what actual people have done and what people actually still do. These are critical stories to tell to enable them to see and face the complexity of moral decision-making in today's complex world.

On a related note, we also need to be specific about the historical violence of the genocide and displacement of Native peoples and the enslavement of African peoples. These are this country's original sins and have set the tone for so much about race and interracial relationships today. Long-term historical learning that starts early builds our kids' capacity to deeply understand how formative these histories and relationships are to the ongoing racial climate in the nation today. So many justice struggles being waged relate directly to these legacies. While our children may not quite understand this yet, building this historical understanding is scaffolding they need to be able to really understand this as they grow.

Meanwhile, we must connect the dots for our children so they see that the same people they learn about in school as heroes and sheroes are the same people who committed this violence. If we don't they are left exposed to internalize views of the United States as a nation innately and exceptionally good, and a pure beacon of equality and justice. The less critical our children are of such a narrative, the more difficult it will be for them to really stand up for justice. Standing up for justice in the United States requires a willingness to challenge myths about this nation that relentlessly circulate in the public square and are simply not true. Exercising their moral muscle by wrestling with complexity is a critically important piece of enabling our kids to hold complicated truths.

There's another developmental gain in the type of exchange I had with H. about Washington, as well. This one may go more unnoticed, but is also of great benefit. Complicating racial history in response to what H. had learned at school planted in her mind the recognition that there may be more to a story (any story) than what she's being told—even if she hears it at school or from someone she trusts.

Before pursuing this discussion, it's worth stating boldly: I deeply value and respect teachers (both generally speaking and my kids' specific ones!). Public educators in the United States do so much with so little and receive woefully less respect and support than is their due.

But school systems in the United States remain embedded in unjust racial structures and teach racial history in ways that perpetuate racial inequity despite the valiant efforts of many good, justice-committed teachers. So we need to teach our kids to question and be appropriately suspicious. If we want white children to be able to ask, challenge, and intervene when injustice is happening, they have to develop the recognition that people in authority positions and with power aren't always correct. We need to position ourselves such that they assume *it's always worth asking whether there is more to the story.* To that end, even though H. was distressed to learn she'd been taught to celebrate the greatness of someone whose willingness to enslave other human beings renders him anything but great, an early lesson in appropriate suspicion is a valuable learning in the journey to effective antiracism.

Supporting Children's Activism

When H. and I discussed George Washington, her question about why we call him good was heartfelt and genuine. By *we*, she almost certainly included her teacher, whom she adored and from whom she had learned about Washington. This was also the point in the exchange that I may have missed an opportunity that would have supported her agency, as well as her sense of vision about the role we can all play in truth-telling and action.

After she and I had explored the question of why we talk about Washington as good, I suggested she could ask her teacher the why question. Given what I knew of her classroom, I knew her teacher would welcome the question and that this would thus be a positive early experience in pushing back on formally conferred knowledge. But H. told me she didn't want to do this.

Despite her declining the invitation, my suggestion further affirmed the validity and importance of her question just by my having made it. It may have also offered her a glimpse of the possibility that she could and can have agency in spaces where an authority figure hasn't taught the whole truth. Moreover, had she taken me up on it, practicing such a response in a space in which I was confident she would be well received would have been a great place to build some of the confidence she will need to engage in other interventions moving forward.

Had H. chosen to take me up on this suggestion, I also suspect her teacher would have responded in a way that generated an important and productive conversation in her classroom. So, in addition to affirming H.'s experience of agency, this would also have positively impacted her classroom environment.

In a different moment, and perhaps even if I could go back in time, I might for any number of reasons have made a different choice than the one I ended up making. Perhaps I should have pushed harder for H. to engage her teacher. Or perhaps I could have tried to pursue the conversation again later with some creative suggestions about how she might do this. Perhaps a role-play exercise, in which we practiced together how she might engage her teacher, would have allowed her to experience the possibility that it would feel good to go back and ask. And, of course, I could have taken this question up with her teacher myself. But while I have certainly done similar things in different moments, this time I didn't pursue it any further. I can't exactly explain why.

Still, a scenario such as this one or countless others similar to it are excellent contexts in which we can encourage our children to see themselves as capable of taking action. As we create opportunities to ask in age-appropriate ways about race and our children's encounters, our children will in turn raise questions and make observations themselves with increasing frequency. And in almost any of these dialogues, agency-inciting visioning becomes possible, as does the possibility for action out of that visioning.

Questions like the following are really helpful:

- How would you have handled "x" if you had been there?
- If you were the person of color in this situation, how do you think you would have wanted a white friend to handle it?
- What do you wish you had said?
- Is there a way you and I could think together about how you might go back and deal with this/find that out/say you disagree?
- Why does that feel hard?
- Would you want to handle an experience like that differently next time?

Each of these questions exercises our children's moral and pragmatic imaginations. They build our relationships as parents who are on a team with them. And they enable opportunities to support our children in following through on insights at which they arrive.

Children are not too young to take action in response to both very specific incidents like the one at H.'s school or larger issues they are coming to some insights about. For example, I recently read an account of a parent supporting a child in writing the Lego company about the lack of Black and brown (and female) figurines in their play sets. What a great example to share with my own children! In a few, but increasingly visible contexts, parents of diverse children are connecting with one another to talk about how they journey with their children in creating a better world. Example after example pops up of children taking action. I am regularly stunned and excited by the ideas parents have for engaging in justice-work with their kids. Connecting with such communities can go a very long way toward enabling us to capitalize on these opportunities with our own children.

Just as we make a habit of reading the news on a regular basis, for example, making a habit of exposing our children to stories like this—stories about youth their own age—is potentially transformative. Just as many of us make a habit of teaching the value of volunteerism and engaging in charitable work (and translating this to make it meaningful for kids), making a habit of translating justice and advocacy work is potentially transformative.

Actions like going back to school to challenge formal knowledge or writing a Lego company that seems to envision Lego people as white and male enables developmental growth that is multilayered. They invite our children to experience a sense of possibility as they acknowledge their own relationship with injustice and choose to act in response to this relationship. These experiences provide them building-block practice in

> Protest is a concrete expression of the belief in justice. It turns the abstract value of justice into a concrete practice.

talking aloud about race and being an advocate for racial justice.

Given how challenging race and antiracism is, and how fraught and loaded are our national contexts, lots of practice from young ages matters. Early work to support healthy white identity development will serve our children well, as taking action gets more difficult and more complicated as they grow. Meanwhile, in regard to all of these distinct areas in which we enable our children to act, we are not only cultivating our children's racial health. We are, more important, participating with them—however slowly—in changing the world.

Protests and Rallies

In the terrain of supporting children's activism, I want to return to the protest story. Earlier I mentioned my awareness that questions emerge around the wisdom of taking our children to protests. I want to circle back to some of these questions. I don't have definitive answers nor am I certain many clear-cut right and wrong positions exist on these questions. But I want to engage some of the ways we might see or respond to the dilemma of taking children to protests.

At this point in our nation's history, protests abound. They'll surely continue to abound for some time. I strongly believe antiracist-committed white Americans have a responsibility to participate in protests. Having said that, then, perhaps the first question is why protests are so important even for adults.

Protests, on their own, don't generate legislative solutions or changes in laws. On their own they may not lead to measurable, concrete outcomes. Meanwhile, protests often attract people well beyond those who are actually willing and able to do the longer, harder, and more tedious work of strategizing and organizing. Sustaining long-term campaigns for social change is hard. Most people don't stay actively in it for the long haul. And so protests can end up bringing together lots of folks who show up for a one-shot event, and then leave feeling good about their contribution but don't do much else. Especially for people doing the longer, harder, more tedious work social transformation requires, that can be really disheartening or even frustrating.

But protests do accomplish many other things. They break public silence and create visibility. As they do so they impact the climate in a local context and put productive pressure on decision-makers in these contexts (as in, "this isn't going to just happen without people raising a fuss"). Enough protests across a nation similarly impact the larger national climate.

The visibility of a protest also creates the possibility of someone at least having to think twice: "What could be so important that people would stand out in the rain on a bridge and yell things?" "Wait! What on earth could be so important that my own neighbor would stand out in the rain on a bridge and yell things?" This type of breaking silence in a community is meaningful.

And something else is certain: when protest is not visible or silence is the strongest sound (the sound that a lack of public, visible protest makes), what gets communicated in a community is that no one cares. What gets communicated is that no one is upset enough to shout aloud and break silence by announcing that things are very, very wrong. Pronounced silence makes us *all* more likely to go along quietly with injustice. That alone is a hugely significant reason to protest.

Protests also change the people who participate in them, and they create connections among folks who see the world in similar ways. In this way they are galvanizing and hope-giving. Physical presence with others who share your values makes it easier for each of us to sustain a practice of justice-oriented resistance for the long haul.

Still, there are many schools of thought on whether or when to take our children to protests and legitimate reasons parents have concerns about doing so. Protests and rallies are usually addressing issues of serious suffering and violence. Parents understandably fear exposing their children—especially younger ones—to such narratives. As one parent ruminated about how much to tell her kids:

> What are the implications of shielding my kid from knowledge of police shootings of African Americans and what are the implications of exposing them to it? It seems like there are risks either way. Sometimes it seems easiest just to put it off until they are older.

This parent was concerned about the potential risk of talking about police violence both in terms of the impact on her own white kids, as well as on kids of color who were friends with her kids. This wasn't a selfish rumination.

This parent wasn't specifically talking about protests. But

her question raises matters germane to the question of children and protests. Namely, kids are going to hear heavy things at rallies and protests. So perhaps we should wait until they are older. Perhaps we should even wait to take them until they can truly choose whether or not they want to go.

Taking this first concern seriously might mean making choices about which rallies we do and don't take our children to. There are ways to involve kids in protest that don't explicitly expose them to overly graphic images or violence. At this point in my children's lives, for example, I will take them to a protest talking about police violence. But I won't take my children to protests that take the form of a die-in.

The latter concern insinuated here in the idea of waiting until kids are older pertains to the recognition that young kids don't yet have deeply informed perspectives. A child is certainly not a fully informed agent and didn't freely choose to be at a protest (or not). Some argue, therefore, that a child at a protest is being used, in a manner of speaking. Meanwhile, it's also true that kids are so cute and compelling that the likelihood a child at a rally is going to attract media attention is high. Kids can seem like they're something of a prop—a way to get extra attention and so, again, being used in a way that should make adults uncomfortable.

I appreciate these concerns and believe the dilemmas are worth taking seriously. And yet the notion of "having an opinion" is not as clear-cut as adults might sometimes think. Many of my nineteen-year-old college students don't really have their own opinion yet. With any luck they'll be sorting this out for years to come. They will come to their own opinions only by being exposed to and engaged with a diverse array of perspectives over time—hopefully with good support. But I still encourage them to go vote.

Meanwhile, parents are always modeling the concrete implications of our values and beliefs for our children. A six-year-old might tell you she believes in kindness. She surely got that belief (and reinforcement for it) from somewhere else. She also might not yet know quite how to use a belief in kindness to concretely negotiate a conflict with an unkind child at school or take some sort of concrete action in response to this belief. This child learns what it means to put the value of kindness into action only as she watches adults in her life model responses to challenges, conflicts, pain, difficult decisions, and uncertainty. Adult behavior turns the abstract value of kindness into concrete practices.

Protest is precisely this type of modeling. Believing in justice is not, in and of itself, an action. Protest is a concrete expression of the belief in justice. It turns the abstract value of justice into a concrete practice. Doing something with our bodies, voices, and in the presence of others is one way we live out our commitment to the value of justice. If we don't model this value it remains at the level of abstraction.

Meanwhile, having our children actually participate in the specific social movements that are unfolding is meaningful to them and to these movements. There's no arguing that Black children played hugely significant roles in the civil rights movement. And, of course, I already suggested that participation in protests is also a powerful way to expose our children to the realities of our local and national racial environments. Participation in protest forms their justice-conscious schemas in deep ways. A central message they begin to internalize is that actual, real people are resisting injustice and speaking up for a better world—that this is something people can, and do, *do*.

Early in life is the time to bring our children into spaces where they watch us, with others, model available and appropriate responses to injustice. The earlier in their lives that they witness and feel the energy and connection of people gathered to raise our voices together and insist things must be changed, the more we build their sense of agency that change is possible.

Obviously, each parent needs to discern for themselves the best choices to make for their children in regard to specific participation or not. I truly don't believe there's one right answer to these questions. But I do believe that asking ourselves honest questions about why we are reluctant to bring children along is important work for us to do as well. Sometimes we may need to rethink the reasons behind our resistance and make sure it keeps us standing on firm antiracist ground.

Resourcing Dissent

The galvanizing connections that can happen when we engage in protests and rallies aren't just useful for our children. They're critical support for us! To that end, a number of activist groups have become larger and powerful in recent years, including groups thinking specifically about white people's role in racial justice and in raising antiracist children. As a result there are activist initiatives conscious about formats for resistance that invite the participation of children.

Showing Up for Racial Justice (SURJ) is a national group composed of local chapters, for example, that engages in many different types of organizing and activism across the nation. SURJ emerged in 2009 in a commitment to bring more white people, in particular, into active support of the Black Lives Matter movement. Members of SURJ have created kid- and parent-specific forums that are robust. These provide significant opportunities for parents of white children to connect and build their capacity. These forums include resource sharing as a way to disseminate models and tools as we try to parent for racial justice. They also include sharing real examples of protests and actions initiated by children and youth, or created with them in mind.

> Visible dissent, sometimes without words, matters when injustice is pervasive. Our kids need to know this.

For example, in the last few years, the San Francisco chapter of SURJ sponsored a multimonth action called Wear It Out Fridays. A youth-led initiative, SURJ supported students who would wear Black Lives Matters T-shirts to school every Friday, talk with others about why they were doing so, and try to increase the numbers of students willing to do the same.

Another resource was created by Black women activists after the 2016 presidential election. The Safety Pin Box came

275

into existence when Marissa Jenae Johnson and Leslie Mac recognized that many white people were bemoaning the state of the nation after the election. Many of these folks were expressing a desire to be in solidarity for justice, but did not have prior experience engaging in antiracist activism.

In the United Kingdom after the Brexit vote, many citizens started wearing safety pins on their clothing to symbolize their dissent from the racial hostility many argued was central in the vote for Brexit. The safety pin signaled that the wearer wanted to be seen as an antiracist and, thus, "safe" person. After the election of Donald Trump to the presidency, a number of Americans began to wear or debate the efficacy of wearing a safety pin—for similar reasons.

Johnson and Mac wanted to push those thinking about wearing a safety pin to take action. This, they believe, is what is really needed in a climate of racial hostility. So branded with the moniker "Effective, Measurable Allyship," they created the Safety Pin Box, which they describe as "The subscription box for white people who want to be allies in the fight for black liberation." Each month a box arrives containing strategies, tools, educational resources, and concrete actions white people can take to grow their antiracist commitment and their skill set.

In summer 2017, the Safety Pin Box unveiled an eight-week summer series for kids. The box set focuses on teaching kids "1) that we need to talk about race and not be afraid of the conversation, and 2) to think about whiteness critically rather than passively accept its privileges."[2] The lessons are designed to bring parents and kids into a journey together. The topics include conversations and exercises oriented around the following—

- **Me:** What does my race mean for me?
- **My Family:** What does race mean for my family?
- **My Community:** How does race affect those in my community and how do I help?
- **The World:** What is Black Lives Matter and where do I fit in?

—and includes resources specifically aimed at enabling children to get active and express their dissent from injustice.[3]

The Safety Pin Box is a resource worth utilizing on its own terms, even beyond the kids series. Parents, teachers, and other caregivers may find it a valuable way to grow our own anti-racist understanding and skill set—especially if activism is not something we've been part of before. But the kid series is particularly brilliant. It's an excellent tool to help us build racial dialogues into the rhythm of our family conversations on a consistent basis. If we've never done that before it can help us begin.

Analyzing the resources to which we can turn to engage our children carefully is an important step in building support for race-conscious parenting. The vast majority of resources intended to engage children in regard to race focus on growing their awareness of and openness to differences. We need resources that are specifically designed, instead, to teach our kids about the power and possibilities of dissent. SURJ and the Safety Pin Box are these kinds of resources.

Justice will not arrive in the United States without massive dissent. Yet so much parenting and schooling and socialization of children focuses on teaching them to do what adults tell them and follow the rules. If we run up against a cultural tendency to be color-blind when we're trying to see and name race, we also run up against a cultural tendency to conform when we need massive dissent from how things are if our commitments to justice are going to be visible. Creating experiential opportunities to make such messages about rule following more complex for our children is key.

The ability to even question *laws* was behind the way we taught our daughter E. to think about immigration. She spends days of her life hearing from us that she is supposed to follow the rules. But now a rule is being used to incite hostility and sometimes violence against people who are racially marginalized. Dissenting from the law, then, is critical for enabling her to reject anti-immigrant discourse.

Similarly, we made sure our children saw images (at the time) of San Francisco Forty-Niner Colin Kaepernick kneeling during the national anthem. When US women's soccer player Megan Rapinoe later followed suit to express solidarity with Kaepernick's dissent, we made sure they saw this as well. We also told them that people were pretty upset with Kaepernick and Rapinoe about these actions.

About this time we were headed as a family to a national women's soccer game. I let both my kids know ahead of time I would be kneeling during the "Star-Spangled Banner." I told them their participation was up to them, and they could choose to kneel or stand. But I made sure they knew why I planned to kneel. Visible dissent, sometimes without words, matters when injustice is pervasive. Our kids need to know this.

These types of experiences aren't all that different from encouraging our kids to ask a critical and suspicious question of their teacher about what they learned at school or from going with them to school to talk to the teacher together. The experience of dissent, of which activism, actions, and protest are a part, enables them to feel the power of standing with others, the challenge and elation of deciding to speak up even when one is alone, and the moral muscle-building that results when we stand up and stand out and say, "This is wrong and we expect better."

Our kids may not end up making the particular types of protest we choose their own. In fact, more likely, they will lead the way with increasingly creative forms of protest. But by engaging them in various kinds of resistance now, they experience and witness dissent as a value. Such observations are deeply informative of their consciousness and their consciences in ways that cannot be overestimated.

Taking Things On at School

Last, but by no means least, it's worth closing out this discussion by returning to the issue of school. We must be prepared to engage our children's schools.

Consider this: if it's difficult to talk openly about race as parents, if the cultural pressure to engage in color-blind approaches is constant, if we don't always know how to go beyond "embrace all differences"—imagine how much more difficult any of this is to do as a teacher. Even if a specific teacher embraces the basic principles of race-consciousness (which some do, but many do not), the pressures teachers face if or as they try to implement such an approach are significant.

Imagine all the white parents who might express concern or even anger when a teacher starts talking about whiteness and complicating George Washington's history! In 2017, journalist Isolde Raftery published an article that showed the e-mails teachers in Seattle Public Schools received from white liberal parents, for example, when the district sponsored a day focused on Black Lives Matter.[4] The anger was intense.

Educating for racial justice takes a brave and deeply empowered teacher. For teachers to be and remain empowered they need vocal and supportive antiracist parents who give them cover and enable them to teach in ways that run up against these broader cultural currents.

Meanwhile, we parents need teachers to be brave and empowered for justice. Our valiant racial justice efforts at home and with kids in our communities are going to be undone, countered, and assailed in their lives at every turn. Good and courageous as our parenting may be, we are only one influence. Our children spend more time in environments outside the home with each passing year of their lives.

Furthermore, our children's learning at school is only partially about what they are formally being taught by other adults. It's also about the countless unsupervised hours they spend learning from their peers (and, vicariously then, from peers' families). So attention to racial learning from school and the racial climates at school are among the most important kinds of attention we can pay. We need to be particularly ready to support and complicate and, when needed, challenge and intervene.

Engaging antiracist commitments at school stands to accomplish many outcomes. Doing so can impact the school's larger environment, making commitments to and questions about antiracism part of the ethos at school. It makes us visible and thus potentially impacts our relationships with other parents there, including with parents of color who experience all kinds of racialized challenges in public school systems. It especially stands to do so when we identify where such parents are already at work engaging the racial climates at school, and step in to support these existing people of color–led efforts first.

And, of course, our children are always watching us. Thus, this is terrain in which we engage in some of the most important and explicit modeling about what it looks like to take a stand for justice in order to impact systems within our spheres of influence.

Having said that, taking up matters at school is almost always difficult. For as many years as I have been doing this work and for as positive, supportive, and wonderful a school as my kids have, one year when one of them came home wearing a feather headdress at Thanksgiving I was really nervous about voicing my distress.

Before talking to her teacher I had to repeatedly practice what I wanted to say. I imagined myself speaking gently and envisioned myself as a player on the same team as her. I thought carefully through my explanations about why a headdress was so problematic in case she didn't immediately see the problem. I practiced my ideas aloud with other adults.

In this particular case, it turns out I didn't need all of that. The conversation went beautifully and the results were effective. My daughter's teacher told me not only had she not been the person who had had the kids make headdresses, but that she had experienced some discomfort about it. She hadn't stopped it, however, because the person who had, had been working really hard and on her own. It felt inconsiderate to step in, then, after the fact and say no.

I appreciated that difficult dilemma. And while it didn't make it okay, I had to admit that I have myself, many times, responded similarly for similar reasons. I've let something pass I knew was wrong. Our dialogue didn't end up making my daughter's teacher defensive or alienating me from the school. On the contrary, besides enabling her fortitude to say headdresses would not be made again in her class, my speaking up enabled her to get more in touch with her desire to not allow something to go forward next time she was uncomfortable. It enabled me to remind myself I have to constantly recommit to doing that as well. In addition, I learned that my child's teacher was open and willing to engage in ways that grew my respect for her.

It's actually not at all uncommon for one white person breaking silence to free others up to do the same. I've learned more than once in my life and in a variety of different contexts that facing my fears and taking on a racist or racialized incident often pays off in ways I didn't imagine it could. It doesn't always happen that way. But it often happens that way.

So when we consider our children's school contexts, it can be useful to assume first that our children's teachers and administrators are on our team and are going to be responsive. We can imagine that other parents share our concerns and longings, and approach them in that spirit. Challenging racism is never easy and it does not always yield the outcomes we are aiming for. But at the same time, we need to know that our verbal, visible, and constructive engagements for justice may very well reveal allies and coparticipants we wouldn't have recognized had we stayed silent or unengaged.

Resistance is a moral value and a lifelong practice. Dissent is a moral value in the context of injustice. Antiracism is a difficult, but utterly humanizing journey. These are not the final words or areas of life in which we need to be courageous journeyers with our children. But these are stories to ponder and postures to try. They are practices to explore and queries to make. As we seek to create a world that is just, we can raise white children who not only learn to long for racial justice, equity, and fairness, but who grow deep commitments to and capacity for calling these into existence. This is a journey with many ongoing unknowns. But it is a journey worth recommitting to every day.

Takeaways

✓ The more we engage our children explicitly about racism and racial injustice, the more often we will find ourselves impressed by their understanding and readiness to act—in spite of the fact that their hearts might be broken by it.

✓ Parents of white children can—and must—step into the unknowns, chart what is mostly still uncharted, and become resilient participants alongside parents of children of color who are already at it and have long been so. A racial justice movement is alive and strong in this nation, and it needs all of us to be *all in*.

✓ The hopes embedded in a commitment to race-conscious parenting require us to allow our children to be vulnerable and feel the ache and hurt of the harm that injustice causes. We may want to insulate our kids from it, but the humanity of even the youngest of our children is directly tied to their ability to identify with that suffering.

✓ Standing up for justice in the United States requires a willingness to challenge relentlessly circulating myths about this nation's history and "heroes" that are simply not true. We must teach kids that it's always worth asking whether there is more to the story, and help them connect the dots.

✓ If we want white children to be able to ask, challenge, and intervene when injustice is happening, they have to develop the recognition that people in authority positions and with power aren't always correct.

✓ It's not at all uncommon for one white person breaking silence to free others up to do the same. Our verbal, visible, and constructive engagements for justice may very well reveal allies and coparticipants we wouldn't have recognized had we stayed silent or unengaged.

A Just Racial Future

One morning in the fall of 2016, I walked away from a school building that was on "external lockdown." My children were inside. This was a totally counterintuitive thing to do as a parent. But that day it seemed to me this had become part of a new normal in the United States.

My kids' school is only ten blocks from where one of two metro-area police officers in Des Moines, Iowa, had been killed in the middle of the night, only hours before the start of the school day. The gunman was still at large. When I had walked into my daughter's classroom at the start of the day, my daughter, who had gotten to her classroom before I did, ran up to me, saying, "Mama, the school doors are locked because a man with a gun killed two police officers last night!"

As I left the school building, I couldn't begin to imagine what these officers' families and loved ones were experiencing in that moment. But I tried to get in touch with what I was feeling.

I was feeling traces of the joy I'd experienced for the first time eight years ago on that very morning as I had held a newborn in my arms. For that same day I walked away from my kids' school with a gunman still at large was the day of my daughter's eighth birthday. And that day began with her talking about guns and killings. So I was also feeling devastation and fear infuse that joy.

> The racial vitriol and violence so publicly on display in this nation with increasing intensity since August 2014 impacts *all of us.*

As news rolled in about the backstory of the alleged gunman (who was arrested shortly after the school day started), I was not the only one struck by the most recent known incident in which he had been involved. Only a few weeks before, this man had waved a Confederate flag in front of a group of Black students at a high school football game during the national anthem. As he was escorted out of the game he had continued in a verbal rampage against the police officers escorting him out, going on about the violation of his rights and wanting his property back.

All I could think was that this horrible day was yet one more symptom of the deep, deadly wound that lies at the heart of this nation. All I could think was that the racial vitriol and violence so publicly on display in this nation with increasing intensity since August 2014 impacts all of us. And all I could think was that our collective lives depended on white people seeing the events of a day like that day in Des Moines in precisely those terms.

The violence of white supremacy always comes back to consume its own. We must understand this. It was horrifying to leave my own children in a school building on lockdown that day. I was saddened, scared, sick, and somber. And I know many of us are similarly somber about the direction in which this nation has seemed to be heading in recent years.

We are all impacted by racism and by racist violence. Whatever the many other factors involved—and there are always many complex factors—the white police officers killed in Des Moines that night and the families devastated in the wake of such unspeakable loss were absolutely the victims of the racism that rolls and churns at the soul of this nation. That violence usually targets people of color, African Americans, immigrants, Native peoples and, increasingly, Muslims. But that day it was obvious that such violence doesn't stop there.

We are a nation that is deeply wounded and engaged in continued wounding. And wounds do not heal without being aired, cleaned, honored in their fullness, and treated. Wounding doesn't stop until it is acknowledged and addressed with honesty; interrupted and repaired.

So it may very well be terrifying to recognize that my children's lives and your children's lives depend on more of us understanding that we are all wounded when we remain in the clutch of that which is unhealed. But I truly and utterly believe that inside that frightening recognition lies great strength, connection, and the possibility of a future. If we can see the stakes, we can find the courage to act.

I hope *Raising White Kids* has helped to jump-start or

further support serious conversation, dialogue, and thinking about active ways in day-to-day life we, as parents, can, literally, change the world. This book, of course, does not presume to be the final word on race-conscious parenting. Nor does it presume to have envisioned every scenario a parent might experience in our radically different and diverse parenting contexts.

But naming and trying to address some of the common paradoxes and challenges that parents of white children experience is a labor of love and an attempt to be part of the movement for liberation. The quandaries we face as parents are real because an unjust system has made them real. And our commitment to create a just system must (and can!) untangle and address these quandaries head-on. Ours is a hope- and freedom-driven parental responsibility.

Real urgency indeed exists about getting serious about this task. A simple, but difficult truth exists at the heart of race-conscious parenting and raising white kids. Namely, being white in a system of white racial hierarchy negatively impacts white people's humanity and health every day, even as it harms and negatively impacts people of color every day. We cannot fully enable children who are white to be healthy until we have created a truly just world.

And so our goal as parents is not—and *must not* simply be—to teach our children to be more inclusive, embracing, and curious humans. These dispositions are important, yes.

But our goal must be to bring them along with us (and, just as likely, to let them bring us along) *as we work to change this world*. Activism is absolutely required.

We are a nation in crisis. Creating a different future requires that we tell the truth about that. Whole communities of children, teenagers, twentysomethings, and beyond are caught in neighborhoods and systems that are heavily patrolled by police, in which there exist school-to-prison pipelines, who are boxed out from high-quality education. Larger-scale social activism must be part of the mix for all white people.

However the various struggles we engage in and commitments we make look, we can and must push back against the silence that pressures us to raise our white children to be good people and just hope for the best. Going in, challenging taboos, speaking against racial dynamics, being brave not only impacts the world we live in, it teaches and equips our children to do the same. Our children can grow into citizens, neighbors, friends, and family members able to resist, dissent, create, and construct as we equip them through race-conscious nurture toward healthy white identity, today, tomorrow, and throughout their lives.

Another world is possible. May it be so.

Acknowledgments

I love to write. And writing is always a vulnerable act. But writing this book has required me to be vulnerable in ways different from and more risky than what I've experienced in any other project.

I've been able to love writing a difficult book and risk vulnerability because of an incredible community of wise people who grace my life. While diverse in the specific ways they support and challenge me, the kind of presence they collectively provide was captured well by my dear friend Rhonda Calderon not so long ago. I was sharing some of my fears and she responded (to paraphrase), "You just need to be clear about what you are doing. Then let the rest go."

I've held on tightly to those words and to those who urge me to keep trying to tell the truth throughout writing *Raising White Kids*.

Lucy Suros continues to be my biggest cheerleader and most faithful friend. She's read and edited at the drop of a hat for years now. She's done so with brilliance and a far more critical eye than my ego usually wants at first. This book literally wouldn't exist in this form without the ways you have pushed, Luce. Melanie Harris and I are sisters from a long, long time ago since. Our scholarly, educational, spiritual, and written (let's do it Rev. Dr. Harris!) collaborations are a source of joy and strength that feed my deepest sense of vocation. Melanie, your belief in me and your willingness to pick up the phone and offer a listening ear, words of wisdom, and prayer remain gifts I still can't quite believe exist in my life. My sister, Janée Harvey, is not only my sister. She's a *heart-soul* friend, a fellow collaborator and activist for racial justice, and, simply put, a rock. She's also a parent whose ways of being with her own kids inspire me. I couldn't do life without you, Ne.

There are many other beloveds here too. Aaron Agne, Miller Hoffman, Shontavia Johnson, Tobi Parks, Bryan Thomas, Darcie Vandegrift, and Aana Vigen are all intellectually engaged friends who enrich my life generally and played different, but essential, roles over the last year of this project. The Crew Scholars at Drake University inspire me everyday, even as they challenge me to be as brave and clear in purpose as they are.

Whatever is good in this book came into the world, in large measure, because of ways those named above have anchored me. Whatever falls short or is inadequate (both are present here) is my responsibility, not theirs.

Catherine Knepper and Calla Devlin Rongerude gave generous professional support as I worked to identify the right publisher. Beth Younger came in with a critical pinch-hit run to the library at an urgent moment. Emily Joye McGaughy, who writes like no other, and Melanie Morrison, whose witness and wisdom have nourished countless resistors at work in the world *today*, came to uniquely sojourn with me over the last year, though I hadn't known them personally before. I could not be more grateful for the real connection now.

I've been so fortunate to work with Roger Freet, my agent. Roger's discerning eye, generosity, and many (many) skills blow my mind. I hope this is just the beginning of what has been an unexpected and delightful partnership. Working with Jamie Chavez, such an excellent editor, has made the hard (and less glamorous) work that comes toward the end of a project lighter and infused with wit. She has also instilled in me a deeper sense of the urgency of this work by her earnest engagement. Susan Salley and Dawn Woods at Abingdon Press have both been outstanding. Susan first recognized the timely need for this book and chose to take the risk. Dawn has engaged countless e-mails, questions, and an author's changing mind with patience and constancy. I have felt such support from the entire Abingdon staff and I appreciate it mightily. Thank you all.

Thanks to the Drake University Center for the Humanities for several different grants at various stages of this long process.

And finally and most important, words to and about my family. We lost our beloved Roka (sweetest boxer ever) during the final week I was writing. Both the pain of that loss, but the precious love and connection we all shared as we said goodbye, are testimony to how primary are the joy, meaning, and stability that my two children, my partner, and our pups bring

293

ACKNOWLEDGMENTS

to my existence. These ones manage to dole out just the right measure: urging me forward daily, while insisting I not take myself too, too seriously. Roka, we all miss you. Cooper and Sukha, thank you for being here. H. and E., I love you and you make me so proud. Chris, there aren't words; I think you already know.

Other Resources

FOR ADULTS ENGAGING WITH KIDS

A select list of online resources and organizations exclusively devoted to supporting adults, with resources, examples, and strategies, to more effectively engage children on race and racial justice.

EMBRACE RACE
www.embracerace.org

Embrace Race is an organization that describes itself as an "online community to discuss and share best practices for raising and caring for kids, all kids, in the context of race."

IN THIS TOGETHER MEDIA
http://inthistogethermedia.com

Focused on increasing the diversity in films and books, In This Together Media creates and highlights stories and titles that put characters who are Black, gay, Muslim, and diverse in many other ways "in the spotlight." It also is engaged in a campaign (#inthistogether) to generate pressure on various media outlets to prioritize diversity.

RAISING RACE CONSCIOUS CHILDREN

www.raceconscious.org

> *Raising Race Conscious Children is an online initiative that offers webinars, blog posts, and a variety of other resources to "support adults who are trying to talk about race with young children." The focus is explicitly on preparing kids to work for racial justice and countering the color-blind framework.*

SHOW UP FOR RACIAL JUSTICE (SURJ)

www.showingupforracialjustice.org

www.showingupforracialjustice.org/tags/families

www.showingupforracialjustice.org/organizing_families

www.showingupforracialjustice.org/surj_families

> *SURJ is an organization devoted to bringing more white people in off the sidelines in active and activist support for people of color–led racial justice organizing. It offers various resources and helps convene a variety of racial justice initiatives, and a number of these are focused on families and children. For example, the "SURJ Families" initiative regularly releases resources for talking about racial justice with our children. Its organizing offers ways to engage in specific racial justice actions as a family and with other families. There are a variety of forums in which parents and teachers committed to raising justice-committed white children can connect, share ideas, participate in conference calls, and access tool kits. A SURJ Parenting Group can be found on Facebook that also provides a way to connect and share resources with other adults committed to racial justice and raising children committed to antiracism.*

THE SAFETY PIN BOX

www.safetypinbox.com

An activist initiative the format of which is monthly subscription, for "white people striving to be allies in the fight for Black Liberation." Offering a variety of tools, The Safety Pin Box has a specific subscription for engaging children and is, itself, a Black-led initiative.

WE NEED DIVERSE BOOKS

http://weneeddiversebooks.org

We Need Diverse Books is a nonprofit organization engaged in a campaign to push the publishing industry to support more diverse books. It also releases an annual list of titles, creates resource lists for where to find more diverse books, and otherwise supports adults in accessing diverse titles for children.

FORUMS FOR ADULTS

A select list of various parenting or education-related forums, which—under their broader mission—have published articles, book lists, toolkits, and other resources for parents.

BRIGHTLY

An organization committed to cultivating lifelong readers

www.readbrightly.com

See, for example, "How to Talk to Kids About Race: Books and Resources that Can Help," by Olugbemisola Rhuday-Perkovich, readbrightly.com/how-to-talk-to-kids -about-race-books-and-resources-that-can-help/

HEALTHYCHILDREN.ORG

American Academy of Pediatrics

www.healthychildren.org

See, for example, "Talking to Children About Racial Bias," by

Ashaunta Anderson and Jacqueline Dougé, healthychildren
.org/English/healthy-living/emotional-wellness/Building
-Resilience/Pages/Talking-to-Children-About-Racial-Bias
.aspx.

TODAY'S PARENT
www.todaysparent.com
See, for example, "How to Talk to Kids About Racism:
An Age-by-Age Guide," by Alex Mlynek, todaysparent
.com/family/parenting/how-to-talk-to-kids-about-racism
-an-age-by-age-guide/.

BOOKS FOR WHITE ADULTS

A select list of resources for adults that focus on white social-
ization, white antiracism, and other specific engagement of
the specific work white people need to do to engage in mean-
ingful racial justice work. Those of us who want to raise
white kids for racial justice need to grow our own under-
standing and practice as well.

Born to Belonging: Writings on Spirit and Justice by Mab Segrest
(New Brunswick, NJ: Rutgers University Press, 2002).
Mab Segrest is a white, lesbian, antiracist activist who has a
long history of powerful racial justice organizing. She is also
an exceptional writer (and currently active with SURJ).

Dear White Christians: For Those Still Longing for Reconciliation
by Jennifer Harvey (Grand Rapids: Eerdmans, 2014).
Provides a clear account of why we still face such racial
division in our faith communities and proposes the response
required from whites who want interracial reconciliation.

Learning to Be White: Money, Race and God in America by Thandeka (New York: Continuum, 1999).

An especially strong, very readable resource by a scholar who is both a theologian (Unitarian Universalist) and psychiatrist.

Memoir of a Race Traitor by Mab Segrest (New York: South End, 1994).

See Born to Belonging above; a powerful account of anti-Klan organizing in the south in the 1980s and the challenges of doing so as a white, lesbian woman.

No Innocent Bystanders: Becoming An Ally in the Struggle for Justice by Shannon Craigo-Snell and Christopher J. Doucot (Louisville: Westminster John Knox, 2018).

A very readable and practical book—written from a Christian perspective but accessible to non-Christians as well. This book draws on the experience and wisdom shared with the authors by activists of color, to offer concrete practices and work that white people can do and need to do to support the justice movements being led by people of color.

A Promise and a Way of Life: White Antiracist Activism by Becky Thompson (Minneapolis: University of Minnesota Press, 2001).

An inspiring historical and sociological investigation into white people who were active in the civil rights movement and who have remained active (often at great personal cost) to today.

Uprooting Racism: How White People Can Work for Racial Justice, rev. ed., by Paul Kivel (Gabriola Island, BC: New Society Publishers, 1996).

This is a great resource for a group to do together (its design lends itself very well to a study session). It's very concrete and practical.

Waking Up White, and Finding Myself in the Story of Race by Debby Irving (Elephant Room Press, 2014).

Highly readable—part memoir, part strategy—with a look at how white people get formed day-to-day; excellent for a group read.

"Why Are All the Black Kids Sitting Together in the Cafeteria?" And Other Conversations About Race by Beverly Daniel Tatum (New York: Basic, 1997).

This book provides a helpful, readable look at how our different racial experiences can lead to breakdowns in communication and trust across racial differences.

Witnessing Whiteness: The Need to Talk About Race and How to Do It by Shelly Tochluk (Lanham, MD: Rowman & Littlefield, 2010).

Highly readable—part memoir, part strategy—this book is honest and compelling.

Notes

1. From Color-Blindness to Race-Conscious Parenting

1. Po Bronson and Ashley Merryman, *NurtureShock: New Thinking About Children* (New York: Twelve, 2009), 54.

2. David J. Kelly et al., "Three-month-olds, but not newborns, prefer own-race faces," abstract, National Center for Biotechnology Information (NCBI), ncbi.nlm.nih.gov/pmc/articles/PMC2566511/ (accessed June 22, 2017).

3. Bronson and Merryman, *NurtureShock*, 54.

4. Rebecca Ulrich and Leila Schochet, "When President Trump Speaks, Our Children Are Listening," Center for American Progress, January 27, 2017, americanprogress.org/issues/early-childhood /news/2017/01/27/297352/when-president-trump-speaks-our-children-are-listening/.

5. Andrew Baron and Mahzarin Banaji, "Evidence of System Justification in Young Children," in *Social and Personality Psychology Compass* 3/6 (2009): 918–26, fas.harvard.edu/~mrb works/articles/2009_Baron_SPPC.pdf.

6. Debra Van Ausdale and Joe R. Feagin, *The First R: How Children Learn Race and Racism* (New York: Rowman & Littlefield, 2001), 104.

7. Ibid., 29.

8. Emma Redden, "Talking with Kids About Racism Is an Act of Kindness and an Act of Freedom," iworeabratogetajob.files.word press.com/2017/06/how-to-talk-to-kids-about-racism_digital _general.pdf (accessed June 30, 2017).

9. Beverly Daniel Tatum, *"Why Are All the Black Kids Sitting Together in the Cafeteria?" and Other Conversations About Race* (New York: Basic, 1997), 6.

10. Van Ausdale and Feagin, *The First R*, 113–14.

11. Bronson and Merryman, *NurtureShock*, 48.

12. Ibid., 43.

13. Tony N. Brown et al., "Child, Parent, and Situational Correlates of Familial Ethnic/Race Socialization," in *Journal of Marriage and Family* 69 (February 2007): 14–25.

14. Tatum, *"Why Are All the Black Kids Sitting Together,"* 52–75.

15. Jesse Rude and Daniel Herda, "Best Friends Forever? Race and the Stability of Adolescent Friendships," in *Social Forces* 89, no. 2 (December 2010): 585–607.

16. Tatum, *"Why Are All the Black Kids Sitting Together,"* 52–75.

17. Bronson and Merryman, *NurtureShock*, 55–62.

18. Daniel Cox, Juhem Navarro-Rivera, and Robert P. Jones, "Race, Religion, and Political Affiliation of American's Core Social Networks," Public Religion Research Institute, August 4, 2018, prri .org/research/poll-race-religion-politics-americans-social-networks/.

19. Ulrich and Schochet, "When President Trump Speaks."

2. Where Do I Start?

1. Debra Van Ausdale and Joe R. Feagin, *The First R: How Children Learn Race and Racism* (New York: Rowman & Littlefield, 2001), 113–14.

2. *Raising Race Conscious Children*, raceconscious.org (accessed July 1, 2017).

3. Po Bronson and Ashley Merryman, *NurtureShock: New Thinking About Children* (New York: Twelve, 2009), 47–52.

4. Kate Ott, *Sex + Faith: Talking with Your Child from Birth to Adolescence* (Louisville: Westminster John Knox, 2013), 41.

5. Yarrow Dunham et al., "Two Signatures of Implicit Intergroup Attitudes: Developmental Invariance and Early Enculturation," in *Psychological Science* 24, no. 6 (June 2013): 860–68.

6. Lin Bian et al., "Gender Stereotypes About Intellectual Ability Emerge Early and Influence Children's Interests," in *Science* 355 (January 27, 2017).

7. Marjorie Rhodes, "Combatting Stereotypes: How to Talk to Your Children," The Conversation, February 15, 2017, theconversation .com/combatting-stereotypes-how-to-talk-to-your-children-71929.

8. Ibid.

9. Ibid.

10. Meghan Holohan, "Friends' Plan to Trick Teacher with Identical Haircuts Is the Sweetest Thing," Today, March 2, 2017, today.com/ parents/boy-wants-haircut-look-his-friend-trick-teacher -t108795.

11. Ibid.

12. Elizabeth A. Harris and Tanzina Vega, "Race in Toyland: A Nonwhite Doll Crosses Over," *New York Times*, July 26, 2014,

303

nytimes.com/2014/07/27/business/a-disney-doctor-speaks-of
-identity-to-little-girls.html.

13. Ibid.

3. What Does a "Healthy" White Kid Look Like?

1. Janet Helms, *A Race Is a Nice Thing to Have: A Guide to Being a White Person or Understanding the White Persons in Your Life*, 2nd ed. (Alexandria, VA: Microtraining Associates, 2007); Beverly Daniel Tatum, *"Why Are All the Black Kids Sitting Together in the Cafeteria?" and Other Conversations About Race* (New York: Basic, 1997).

2. Helms, *A Race Is a Nice Thing to Have*, 30.

3. Tim Wise, *Between Barack and a Hard Place: Racism and White Denial in the Age of Obama* (San Francisco: City Lights, 2009).

4. Tatum, *"Why Are All the Black Kids Sitting Together,"* 10.

5. Catherine Fosl, *Subversive Southerner: Anne Braden and the Struggle for Racial Justice in the Cold War South* (Louisville: University Press of Kentucky, 2006), 331.

4. Do We Have to Call It Racism?

1. Kimberly Chang and Rachel Conrad, "Following Children's Lead in Conversations About Race," in *Everyday Antiracism: Getting Real About Race in School*, ed. Mica Pollock (New York: New Press, 2008), 36.

2. Ibid.

3. Ibid., 37.

4. Ibid., 34.

5. Glenn E. Singleton and Cyndie Hays, "Beginning Courageous Conversations About Race," in *Everyday Antiracism*, 19.

6. Chang and Conrad, "Following Children's Lead," 34.

7. Tatum, *Why Are All the Black Kids Sitting Together,* 4.

8. Po Bronson and Ashley Merryman, *NurtureShock: New Thinking About Children* (New York: Twelve, 2009), 64.

9. Ibid.

10. Ibid., 63.

11. Rumaan Alam, "We Don't Only Need More Diverse Books. We Need More Books Like *The Snowy Day*," *Slate*, August 2, 2016, slate.com/blogs/nightlight/2016/08/02/ezra_jack_keats_the_snowy_day_is_a_model_for_treating_black_characters_in.html (accessed July 1, 2017).

5. Our Bodies in Racial Scripts

1. Daniel Cox, Juhem Navarro-Rivera, and Robert P. Jones, "Race, Religion, and Political Affiliation of American's Core Social Networks," Public Religion Research Institute, August 4, 2018, prri.org/research/poll-race-religion-politics-americans-social-networks/.

2. Phillip Atiba Goff et al., "The Space Between Us: Stereotype Threat and Distance in Interracial Contexts," in *Journal of Personality and Social Psychology* 94, no. 1 (2008): 91.

3. Ibid., 91–98.

4. Shannon Sullivan, *Revealing Whiteness: The Unconscious Habits of Racial Privilege* (Bloomington and Indianapolis: Indiana University Press, 2006), 3.

5. Ibid., 10.

6. Anna Olson, "The Only White Kid in the Room," August 26, 2013, livingformations.com/2013/08/26/the-only-white-kid-in-the-room/ (accessed July 4, 2017).

7. Sullivan, *Revealing Whiteness*, 10.

6. Diversity Is Confusing!

1. Mary Bucholtz, *White Kids: Language, Race, and Styles of Youth Identity* (Cambridge: Cambridge University Press, 2011), xi.

2. Ibid., 211.

3. Ibid., 232–34.

4. Denise Oliver Velez, "Joan Trumpauer Mulholland: The Civil Rights Activist You May Not Know About," Daily Kos, April 30, 2017, dailykos.com/story/2017/4/30/1654976/-Joan-Trumpauer -Mulholland-the-civil-rights-activist-you-may-not-know-about (accessed July 2, 2017).

5. Debra Van Ausdale and Joe R. Feagin, *The First R: How Children Learn Race and Racism* (New York: Rowman & Littlefield, 2001), 208.

6. Beverly Daniel Tatum, *"Why Are All the Black Kids Sitting Together in the Cafeteria?" and Other Conversations About Race* (New York: Basic, 1997), 11–12.

7. "Illustrating Equity VS Equality," Interaction Institute for Social Change, January 13, 2016, interactioninstitute.org/illustrating -equality-vs-equity/ (accessed July 2, 2017).

7. What Does Resistance Look Like?

1. The Michigan Conference of the United Church of Christ General Assembly, October 2017, Flint, Michigan.

2. The Safety Pin Box, safetypinbox.com/kids (accessed July 1, 2017).

3. Ibid.

4. Isolde Raftery, "To Understand White Liberal Racism Read These Private Emails," KUOW, July 16, 2017, kuow.org/post/under stand-white-liberal-racism-read-these-private-emails (accessed July 5, 2017).